CRACKING CLINICAL SAS INTERVIEWS EASY WAY

REAL TIME PROJECT RELATED AND TECHNICAL SHORT Q&A GUIDE

SHIVA RAVINDRA

Welcome to '*Cracking Clinical SAS Interviews*'! As *Shiva Ravindra, known by my pen name*, a seasoned expert in clinical SAS programming with over 15 years of experience.

With my wife's **Ramya** support, I've distilled years of expertise into 150 crucial Q&A to help you excel in interviews. Whether you're a beginner or a seasoned pro, this book is your definitive companion on the journey to mastering clinical SAS interviews. Dive in, and let's unlock the secrets to your interview success together

Dive into interview success with 'Cracking Clinical SAS Interviews'

To my wife: my strength, my guiding light, and my unwavering support on life's journey, this book is dedicated to you.

The first step is always the hardest, but it's also the most rewarding.

Contents

Contents

Contents

Contents

Contents

How to Craft the Perfect Clinical SAS Programmer Resume: Expert Insights Unveiled?

Name :
<u>Email id :</u>
+91 mobile number :

<u>**Professional Summary:**</u>

- Having **10+ years of experience** in **SAS programming** with strong emphasis on analysis of Clinical Trial projects in Pharmaceutical and Healthcare Industry.
- Proficiency in SAS/Base, SAS/Macros, SAS ODS on windows, Unix environment (SAS through SAS9.2,9.3 and 9.4)
- Assist group leader on project management which includes scheduling of the project work, workload allocation for programming team members and timeline management.
- Attend project team meetings, provide technical advice to the team on work plan.
- Generated **SDTM, ADaM, Tables and Listings** as per company standards and in compliance with FDA and other regulatory compliance.
- Have experience in creating competing validation programs for analysis datasets and reports (TLF's).
- Provide technical support to other SAS programmers for coding and debugging.
- Familiar with CDISC standards and clinical trials methodology.
- Extensive experience in **Phase I, Phase II, III and IV** clinical trial studies in different therapeutic areas.
- Excellent in analytical, presentation, communication and problem solving skills and work independently as well as in a team
- Good understanding of CDISC, SDTM models.
- Experienced in producing **RTF, PDF** formatted files using SAS ODS facility.
- Good understanding of Clinical Trials research methodologies.
- Experienced in UNIX environment/commands and shell scripts.

<u>**Professional Skills**</u>
SAS Skills
BASE-SAS, SAS/MACRO, SAS/STAT, SAS/SQL, SAS/GRAPH, SAS/ACCESS, SAS Enterprise Guide.
Databases
Oracle , Rave
Programming Languages
SQL & R
CDISC

SDTM, ADaM
Operating Systems
Windows 7/10, Unix , Entimice,BCE
Education
Bachelor of Pharmacy xxxxx University in xxxx.
Master of Pharmacy xxxxxxx University in xxxx.
Professional Experience
Currently working as, a **Senior Statistical Programmer** in **xx,** Home based since Dec2021 to till date.

....
RECENT PROJECTS:
Project-01 Title:
A Double-Blind Placebo-Controlled Study to Assess the Efficacy and Safety of Oral Active Drug versus Placebo in Patients with Mild to Moderate COVID-19 Disease
Role : Prinical programmer (FTE)
Responsibilities:

- Developed and validated ADaM datasets tables and listings in alignment with the SAP and mock shells
- Provided technical advice during project team meetings, contributing to effective work/ timeline planning
- Documented and tracked project-related progress, ensuring accurate records
- Assisted group leader in project management, including scheduling, workload allocation, and timeline management
- Played a key role in ensuring smooth project workflow and adherence to timelines
- Applied advanced SAS programming skills to produce ADaM'S, tables, listings, and Figures from clinical trial data
- Updated ADaM specifications in compliance with evolving CDISC standards
- Collaborated effectively with the Data Management department, addressing data-related challenges, and developing offline listings
- Worked on P21 and Define.xml packages, contributing to comprehensive data presentation and metadata definition
- Engaged in the development of Analysis Data Reviewer's Guide (ADRG) and Submission Data Reviewer's Guide (SDRG), contributing to comprehensive data presentation and effective analysis
- Responsible for conducting statistical programming package reviews before delivery to the customer

Project -02 Title:
A multicenter, randomized, double-blinded, crossover, placebo-controlled Phase II study to assess the effect of Active drug versus placebo on high-sensitivity cardiac troponin I (hs-cTnI) release in patients with chronic heart failure after exercise when used in addition to standard of care
Role : Project lead (SLP)
Responsibilities:

- Leveraged advanced SAS programming expertise to adeptly create Analysis Data Sets (ADaM'S), Tables, Listings and Figures derived from complex clinical trial data
- Actively participated in the iterative refinement of ADaM specifications, consistently aligning them with evolving CDISC standards and Trial Level Summaries (TLF's) for enhanced data interpretation
- Coordinated seamlessly with the Data Management department to address intricate data challenges and collaborate on the creation of offline listings, fostering a cohesive approach to data-related matters
- Provided valuable technical support to fellow SAS programmers, facilitating efficient coding and comprehensive debugging procedures

- Demonstrated a solid understanding of CDISC standards and adeptly applied clinical trials methodology, resulting in meticulous data handling and maintenance of quality standards
- Responsible for conducting statistical programming package reviews before delivery to the customer

Project-03 Title:

An open label, balanced, randomized, two-treatment, two-period, two-sequence, single dose, crossover, oral bioequivalence study of Active Drug Tablets 10 mg with Refrence Drug ® Tablets 10 mg in healthy, adult, human subjects under fasting conditions.
Role : Senior programmer
Responsibilities:

- Developing ADaM dataset as pre-specification and review
- Developing tables and listings as per SAP and mock shells
- Conduct project team meetings. Provide technical advice to the team on work plan
- Documentation and tracking of project related work progress
- Assist group leader on project management which includes scheduling of the project work, workload allocation for programming team members, and timeline management
- Provide SAS programming expertise in producing ADS, Tables and Listings from clinical trial data.
- Generate reports, listings using SAS/BASE and SAS/MACRO SAS/SQL and SAS/STAT.
- Updating ADaM spec as per CDISC Requirements and TLF's
- Coordinated with DM department on data issues and offline listings

Project-04 Title:

Phase 1 Trial of Intralesional Immunotherapy with Active Drug 2.0 Vaccine in Patients with Advanced Merkel Cell Carcinoma or Cutaneous Squamous Cell Carcinoma
Role : Senior programmer
Responsibilities:

- Provide SAS programming expertise in producing, ADS, Tables and Listings from clinical trial data.
- Conduct project team meetings. Provide technical advice to the team on work plan
- Documentation and tracking of project related work progress
- Create macros and use existing macros to develop SAS programs for clinical data analysis.

Project-05 Title:

Oncology
A Phase-2 Study of ENZASTAURIN in Patients with Relapsed Cutaneous T-cell Lymphoma
Role : Senior programmer
Responsibilities:

- Provide SAS programming expertise in producing, ADS, Tables and Listings from clinical trial data.
- Conduct project team meetings. Provide technical advice to the team on work plan
- Documentation and tracking of project related work progress
- Create macros and use existing macros to develop SAS programs for clinical data analysis.

Environment: SAS 9.1.3/9.2,9.3,9.4, Base SAS, SAS Macros, SAS SQL, SAS STAT, MS Office, Windows.

CHAPTER TWO

What is your roles and responsibilities and day to day activities?

1. Leveraged advanced SAS programming expertise to adeptly create Analysis Data Sets (ADaM's), Tables, Listings, and Figures derived from complex clinical trial data.

2. Actively participated in the iterative refinement of ADaM specifications, consistently aligning them with evolving CDISC standards and Trial Level Summaries (TLF's) for enhanced data interpretation.

3. Coordinated seamlessly with the Data Management department to address intricate data challenges and collaborate on the creation of offline listings, fostering a cohesive approach to data-related matters.

4. Provided valuable technical support to fellow SAS programmers, facilitating efficient coding and comprehensive debugging procedures.

5. Demonstrated a solid understanding of CDISC standards and adeptly applied clinical trials methodology, resulting in meticulous data handling and maintenance of quality standards.

6. Responsible for conducting statistical programming package reviews before delivery to the customer.

7. Collaborated effectively with cross-functional teams to ensure alignment between programming activities and project timelines.

8. Implemented innovative solutions to streamline data processing and analysis procedures, improving efficiency and accuracy.

9. Actively participated in continuous learning and development activities to stay abreast of emerging trends and best practices in clinical SAS programming.

10. Contributed to the development and enhancement of internal processes and procedures to optimize workflow efficiency and ensure adherence to regulatory requirements.

11. Developed and implemented standardized programming macros and utilities to expedite repetitive tasks and enhance productivity across projects.

12. Played a key role in the design and implementation of data validation checks to ensure the accuracy and integrity of clinical trial data, minimizing errors and discrepancies.

13. Collaborated closely with statisticians to generate statistical analysis datasets and provide programming support for statistical analyses, contributing to the overall success of clinical studies.

14. Actively participated in regulatory agency inspections and audits, providing programming support and contributing to the preparation and review of documentation as needed.

15. Demonstrated strong problem-solving skills by identifying and resolving programming issues and data discrepancies in a timely manner, ensuring project timelines and deliverables were met.

16. Provided training and mentorship to junior team members, sharing best practices and fostering their professional growth and development in clinical SAS programming.

17. Acted as a subject matter expert (SME) on CDISC standards and regulatory requirements, providing guidance and recommendations to ensure compliance and adherence to industry standards.

18. Collaborated with cross-functional teams to develop data visualization tools and dashboards to facilitate data review and decision-making processes for clinical trial management.

CHAPTER THREE

What is your study title and primary and secondary objective and endpoints?

In short, objectives outline the overall goals of a clinical trial, while endpoints are specific outcomes measured to assess the effect of the intervention being studied.

<u>Project-01:</u> *COVID-19*

Infection and infestation therapeutic area

A Double-Blind Placebo-Controlled Study to Assess the Efficacy and Safety of Oral C-Drug Versus Placebo in Patients with Mild to Moderate COVID-19 Disease

The primary objective is to **determine if C-Drug (AA) increases the proportion of patients** with **clinical recovery** from COVID-19symptoms on Day 14 in patients with mild to moderate COVID-19 disease compared with placebo.

Clinical recovery on Day 14 is defined as:

- Temperature ≤ 37.7°C (oral or skin surface)
- Respiratory rate ≤ 24/minute on room air
- Shortness of breath – absent
- Cough – mild or absent on a patient-reported scale

Secondary objectives are to determining:

- Decreases the hospitalization rate due to COVID-19 by Day 14
- Decreases the number of medical follow-up visits by Day 14
- Increases the proportion of patients with absence of clinical symptoms byindividual symptom at Day 14 (this includes the symptoms included in theprimary endpoint of clinical recovery as well as other symptoms on the 14Common COVID-19-Related Symptoms Severity Scale

Description of the Study

This study is a double-blind, randomized, multisite, placebo-controlled trial comparing the safety and efficacy of AA with placebo in non-hospitalized patients with mild to moderate COVID-19 disease. Approximately 275 patients with COVID-19 will be enrolled with the goal of reaching 250 randomized patients who completed the study.

Primary Efficacy Endpoint

Proportion of patients with **clinical recovery** of COVID-19 symptoms on Day 14 (±1 day), where clinical recovery on Day 14 is defined as:

- Temperature ≤ 37.7°C (oral or skin surface)
- Respiratory rate ≤ 24/minute on room air

- Shortness of breath – absent
- Cough – mild or absent on a patient-reported scale

A patient will be considered a clinical failure if lost to follow-up (LTFU) or hospitalized for treatment of COVID-19 disease even if the above conditions meet on Day 14.

Secondary Efficacy Endpoints

- **Hospitalization rates** due to COVID-19 symptoms (excluding non-COVID 19 causes including admittance for other upper respiratory infections and admittance only for administrative or observations purposes)
- **Number of COVID-19-related medical follow up visits** (Doctor's office or emergency room (ER) visit)
- **Proportion of patients with COVID-19 symptoms** at Day 14 by individual symptom (this includes the symptoms included in the primary endpoint of clinical recovery as well as other symptoms on the 14 Common COVID-19-Related Symptoms Severity Scale)

Exploratory Efficacy Endpoints

- **Time to maximum severity** of COVID-19 symptoms after start of treatment
- **Time to resolution of COVID-19** symptoms including cough, fever, shortness of breath and elevated respiratory rate.
- **Proportion of patients clinically recovered** at Day 28 (± 1 day)
- **Log viral load reduction as measured by quantitative RT-PCR** at Day 5 compared with baseline
- **Cytokine and chemokine levels at Screening**, Day 5 and Day 14
- Anti-SARS-CoV-2 antibody levels (IgM and IgG) at Screening and Day 14

Safety Endpoints

- Adverse events (AEs) and serious adverse events (SAEs)
- Vital signs (heart rate and blood pressure)
- Clinical chemistry and hematology

<u>**Project-02:**</u>
Therapeutic area: cardiovascular
A multicenter, randomized, double-blinded, crossover, placebo-controlled Phase II study to assess the effect of serelaxin versus placebo on high-sensitivity cardiac troponin I (hs-cTnI) release in patients with chronic heart failure after exercise when used in addition to standard of care/
Primary Objective:
Assess the effect of serelaxin versus placebo on high-sensitivity cardiac troponin I (hs-cTnI) release in patients with chronic heart failure after exercise.
Secondary Objective:
Evaluate the safety and efficacy of serelaxin compared to placebo when used in addition to standard of care.
Measure additional biomarkers or clinical parameters related to heart failure in response to serelaxin treatment.
Assess the impact of serelaxin on patient-reported outcomes or quality of life measures.

Primary Endpoint:

- The primary endpoint was the analysis of efficacy variables, including NT-proBNP, H-FABP, hs-cTnT, echocardiogram assessment, spirometry, and ergometry assessments.

Secondary Endpoints:

- Secondary endpoints include the analysis of additional parameters such as specific biomarkers (NT-proBNP, H-FABP, hs-cTnT), echocardiogram parameters, spirometry, ergometry assessments, and the Borg CR10 scale to measure the intensity of experiences.

In this study:

- The primary analysis using a **mixed model repeated measures** was canceled due to an inadequate sample size.

- Instead, primary and other efficacy endpoints will be summarized using standard descriptive statistics.

- Parameters specified later will be analyzed using a Student's t-test.

- All analyses will be conducted on the FAS population.

- For NT-proBNP, the weighted mean log-transformed concentration values will be compared between treatments using a Student's t-test. Treatment difference, confidence interval, and p-value will be provided. Additionally, raw assay concentrations will be summarized descriptively.

- Similar analysis will be conducted for H-FABP, comparing weighted mean log-transformed concentration values between treatments using a Student's t-test, and raw assay concentrations will be summarized similarly to NT-proBNP.

Project-03:

BA/BE study

An open label, balanced, randomized, two-treatment, two-period, two-sequence, single dose, crossover, oral bioequivalence study of Succinate Tablets 10 mg with CARE®(Succinate) Tablets 10 mg in healthy, adult, human subjects under fasting conditions.

Primary Objective:

- To assess the bioequivalence of Solifenacin Succinate Tablets 10 mg from airis PHARMA Private Limited, India, with CARE® (Succinate) Tablets 10 mg from Pharma US, Inc., Northbrook, IL , in healthy adult human subjects under fasting conditions.

Secondary Objective:

- To monitor adverse events and ensure the safety of subjects.

Primary Endpoints:

- Pharmacokinetic Parameters:
- Cmax (maximum plasma concentration)
- AUC0-72 (area under the plasma concentration-time curve from time zero to 72 hours)

Secondary Endpoint:

- Pharmacokinetic Parameter:
- Tmax (time to reach maximum plasma concentration)

Bioequivalence Criteria:

- The test (T) product is considered bioequivalent to the reference (R) if the 90% two one-sided confidence interval for the difference of the least square means of the logarithmic transformed values of Cmax and AUC0-72 is between 80.00% and 125.00% for Solifenacin.

Project-04:

Oncology

Phase 1 Trial of Intralesional Immunotherapy with IFx-Hu2.0 Vaccine in Patients with Advanced Merkel Cell Carcinoma or Cutaneous Squamous Cell Carcinoma

Primary Objective:

- To assess the safety of vaccinating with intralesional IFx-Hu2.0 therapy in patients with Merkel cell carcinoma (MCC) or cutaneous squamous cell carcinoma (cSCC).

Secondary Objectives:

- To assess the feasibility of IFx-Hu2.0 administration.
- To evaluate preliminary efficacy of IFx-Hu2.0.

Exploratory Objectives:
- To evaluate immune response via biomarkers.

Primary Endpoint:
- Safety, defined as the absence of dose-limiting toxicities (DLTs), which is the absence of any grade 3-5, treatment-related Adverse Events (AEs) per Common Terminology Criteria for Adverse Events (CTCAE) v5.0 from the first injection (Day 1) to final follow-up (Day 28, 35, or 42 depending on dosing schedule) ± 7 days.

Secondary Endpoints:
- Feasibility, defined as study completion by ≥80% of patients (i.e., 16/20) in the per-protocol analysis.
- Preliminary treatment response, measured by Overall Response Rate (ORR).

Exploratory Endpoint:
- Tumor-specific immune response, measured by laboratory tests of correlative studies.

<u>**Project-05**</u>

Oncology

Title:

A Phase-2 Study of ENZASTAURIN in Patients with Relapsed Cutaneous T-cell Lymphoma

Primary Objective:
- To evaluate the safety and efficacy of ENZASTAURIN in patients with relapsed cutaneous T-cell lymphoma (CTCL).

Secondary Objectives:
- To assess the feasibility of ENZASTAURIN administration.
- To determine the overall objective tumor responsive rate of ENZASTAURIN in patients with relapsed CTCL.
- To monitor the length and intensity of exposure to study medication.
- To evaluate adverse events associated with ENZASTAURIN treatment.
- To conduct physical examinations and monitor vital signs.
- To assess laboratory tests, including ECG and ECOG.

Primary Endpoint: Determine the response rate using standardized criteria, including Complete Response (CR), Partial Response (PR), Stable Disease (SD), and Progressive Disease (PD).

Secondary Endpoints:
- Feasibility, defined as study completion by ≥80% of patients (i.e., 16/20) in the per-protocol analysis.
- Overall objective tumor responsive rate, measured by evaluating the reduction in tumor size or stabilization of tumor growth using standardized criteria such as RECIST.
- Length and intensity of exposure to study medication, determined by the duration and dosage of ENZASTAURIN administration.
- Adverse events, including the incidence and severity of treatment-related adverse events.
- Physical examination findings, including any changes in the patient's overall health status or specific symptoms related to CTCL.
- Vital signs monitoring, assessing changes in blood pressure, heart rate, temperature, and respiratory rate throughout the study period.
- Laboratory test results, including ECG to monitor cardiac function and ECOG to assess performance status.

PROJECT-06:

IMMUNOLOGY:

Multiple Phase 2b Studies Evaluating the Efficacy and Safety of ACTIVE DRUG for the Treatment of Participants with Moderate to Severe Psoriasis

- Primary Objectives

- To evaluate the dose response of JNJ-77242113 at Week 16 in participants with moderate-to-severe plaque psoriasis
- Primary Endpoint
- Proportion of participants achieving PASI 75 (≥75% improvement from baseline in PASI) at Week 16

- To evaluate the dose response of JNJ-77242113 at Week 16 in participants with moderate-to-severe plaque psoriasis
- Primary Endpoint

Which datasets are utilized and methods used to meet the primary and secondary goals and endpoints effectively?

Project-01: *COVID-19*

The primary objective is to **determine if C-Drug (AA) increases the proportion of patients** with **clinical recovery** from COVID-19symptoms on Day 14 in patients with mild to moderate COVID-19 disease compared with placebo.

```
Table 14.2.1.1 Analysis of Clinical Recovery Rate of COVID-19 Symptoms with a 2x2 Contingcy Table
                                    ITT Population


  Definition / rate                                   Tafenoquine              Placebo
     Statistic                                          (N=xxx)                (N=xxx)


  Clinical Recovery of COVID-19 Symptoms on Day 14
      n (%)                                             n (xx.x)               n (xx.x)
      95% CI for Clinical Recovery Rate[a]          (xx.xx, xx.xx)         (xx.xx, xx.xx)
      p-value (vs. placebo) [b]                        0.xxxx

  Clinical Recovery of COVID-19 Symptoms on Day 28
      n (%)                                             n (xx.x)               n (xx.x)
      95% CI for Clinical Recovery Rate[a]          (xx.xx, xx.xx)         (xx.xx, xx.xx)
      p-value (vs. placebo) [b]                        0.xxxx

  % is based on ITT population. CI = Confidence Interval.
  [a] Copper-Pearson exact 95% CI
  [b] p-value is provided by Fisher Exact test
```

Clinical recovery on Day 14 Flag *COVD14FL*

If the subject met all the Clinical Recovery conditions as per SAP at Day 14 then flag as 'Y'; Else Set to 'N'

Clinical recovery on Day 14 is defined as:

- Temperature ≤ 37.7°C (oral or skin surface)
- Respiratory rate ≤ 24/minute on room air
- Shortness of breath – absent
- Cough – mild or absent on a patient-reported scale

SAS CODING:
data COVD14FL;
set adam.adsl;
where ittfl = 'Y' and trt01an ne .;
*if **COVD14FL**="Y" then COVD14FLn=**1**;*
*else if COVD14FL in("N","") then COVD14FLn=**2**;*

run;
PROCSORT *DATA = COVD14FL; BY trt01an;* **RUN;**
/ Assumption that the response of interest we are interested in is the lower value 1 (i.e. yes = 1 and 2 = no */*
ODS TRACE ON;
ODS OUTPUT BinomialCLs=CI14;
PROCFREQ *DATA = COVD14FL;*
BY trt01an;
TABLES COVD14FLn/BINOMIAL (EXACT) ALPHA = **0.05** *MISSPRINT out=N14;*
/ WEIGHT COUNT;*/*
ODS OUTPUT Freq.ByGroup1.Table1.BinomialCLs = Clopper1;/ Clopper-Pearson 95% Exact CI for Treatment 1 */*
ODS OUTPUT Freq.ByGroup2.Table1.BinomialCLs = Clopper2; / Clopper-Pearson 95% Exact CI for Treatment 2 */*
run;
ODS TRACE ON;
PROCFREQ *DATA = COVD14FL;*
*TABLES COVD14FLn*trt01an/EXACT;*
/ WEIGHT COUNT;*/*
ODS OUTPUT Freq.Table1.FishersExact = FishersExact14;
RUN;
DATA *Pval14;*
SET FishersExact14;
WHERE NAME1 IN ('XP2_FISH'); / CVALUE is the p-value from the two-sided test to include in Table */*
c0=" p-value (vs. placebo) [b]";
*c1=strip(put(cValue1,**6.4**));*
*ord1=**1**;*
*ord2=**4**;*
keep c0 c1 ord1 ord2;
RUN;
ODS TRACE OFF;

<u>Project-02:</u>
Therapeutic area: cardiovascular
Primary Objective:
Assess the effect of serelaxin versus placebo on high-sensitivity cardiac troponin I (hs-cTnI) release in patients with chronic heart failure after exercise.

Primary Endpoint:
- The primary endpoint was the **analysis of efficacy variables**, including NT-proBNP, H-FABP, hs-cTnT, echocardiogram assessment, spirometry, and ergometry assessments.

Cardiac troponin is the preferred biomarker for the diagnosis of acute myocardial infarction (AMI).

the primary analysis of **mixed model repeated measures** *will not be performed.*

Primary and other efficacy endpoints will be summarized using standard descriptive statistics.

Further selected parameters (as specified in later sections) will be analyzed using a **Student's t-test.**

Analysis of NT-proBNP
Analysis of H-FABP
Analysis of echocardiogram assessment

Analysis of spirometry and ergometry assessments

A test for B-type natriuretic peptide (BNP) or N-terminal pro b-type natriuretic peptide (**NT-proBNP**) is primarily used to help detect, diagnose, and evaluate the severity of heart failure.

SAS CODE:

```
ods trace on;
   ods output diffs=diff ;
   ods output LSMeans=lsm ;
   procmixed data=main;
   by paramn;
   class seq avisitn TRT;
   model aval2= seq avisitn TRT;
   /*The MODEL statement names a single dependent variable and the fixed effects, which determine the matrix of the
mixed model (see the section Parameterization of Mixed Models for details). The specification of effects is the same as in
the GLM procedure; however, unlike PROC GLM, you do not specify random effects in the MODEL statement. The MODEL
statement is required.*/
   /*lsmeans trt / pdiff cl;*/
   /*he LSMEANS statement computes least squares means (LS-means) of fixed effects.*/
   /*estimate 'A Serelaxin vs Placebo' trt -1 1/ cl;*/
   run;
   ;
   procttest data=main ;
   by paramn;
   class trt;
   var aval2 ;
   ods output statistics=result2 (keep=paramn CLASS);
   run;
   ods trace off;
```

The TTEST Procedure

Variable: Height

Species	Method	N	Mean	Std Dev	Std Err	Minimum	Maximum
1		12	17.0000	2.2962	0.6629	13.0000	21.0000
2		12	19.3333	3.0551	0.8819	15.0000	24.0000
Diff (1-2)	Pooled		-2.3333	2.7024	1.1033		
Diff (1-2)	Satterthwaite		-2.3333		1.1033		

Species	Method	Mean	95% CL Mean		Std Dev	95% CL Std Dev	
1		17.0000	15.5410	18.4590	2.2962	1.6266	3.8987
2		19.3333	17.3922	21.2744	3.0551	2.1642	5.1871
Diff (1-2)	Pooled	-2.3333	-4.6213	-0.0453	2.7024	2.0900	3.8249
Diff (1-2)	Satterthwaite	-2.3333	-4.6316	-0.0350			

Method	Variances	DF	t Value	Pr > |t|
Pooled	Equal	22	-2.11	0.0460
Satterthwaite	Unequal	20.422	-2.11	0.0469

Project-03:

BA/BE study

Primary Objective:

- To assess the bioequivalence of Succinate Tablets 10 mg from airis PHARMA Private Limited, India, with CARE® (Succinate) Tablets 10 mg from Pharma US, Inc., Northbrook, IL , in healthy adult human subjects under fasting conditions.

Primary Endpoints:

- Pharmacokinetic Parameters:
- Cmax (maximum plasma concentration)
- AUC0-72 (area under the plasma concentration-time curve from time zero to 72 hours)

Section 14.2: Efficacy/Pharmacodynamic/Pharmacokinetic Data

Table 14.2.1 Summary of <Analyte> Plasma Concentrations versus Nominal Sampling Times by Treatment (Pharmacokinetic Population)

Nominal Time Point	Statistic	Test (N = XX)	Reference (N = XX)
Pre-dose	n	XX	XX
	Arithmetic Mean	XX.X	XX.X
	SD	XX.XX	XX.XX
	Median	XX.X	XX.X
	Minimum	XX.X	XX.X
	Maximum	XX.X	XX.X
	CV%	XX.XX	XX.XX
	Geometric Mean	XX.X	XX.X

Table 14.2.3 Statistical Analysis of <Analyte> Pharmacokinetic Parameters (Pharmacokinetic Population)

Comparison	Parameter (Unit)	N	LSMeans Reference	Test	% Ratio (Test/Reference)	90% Confidence Interval of Ratio	Intra CV	Inter CV	Power
Test vs. Reference	Cmax (Unit)								
	AUC0-t (Unit)								
	AUCinf (Unit)								

ods trace on;
ods output LSMeans= LSMeans;
ods output Diffs=Diffs;
ods output Estimates= Estimates;
ods output CovParms= CovParms;
;
PROCMIXED *data=pkparm;*
CLASS seqence subno period treat ;
MODEL lcmax = treat period/solution
ddfm=satterth;

RANDOM subno(seqence);
LSMEANS treat / PDIFF CL alpha=0.10;
estimate 'T/R' treat -11 / cl alpha=0.10;
run;
** Anti-log transformation to obtain the ratio of Geometric Means (point estimate) and its 90% confidence interval (lower and upper bounds);*
***data** diffs2;*
set Estimates;
*gmean=exp(estimate); *Geometric means;*
*ratio=exp(estimate); ** Ratio of geometric mean;*
*lower=exp(Lower); ** 90% CI lower bound;*
*upper=exp(upper); ** 90% CI upper bound;*
Comp="cmax ";
run;

This SAS code appears to be conducting an analysis of variance (ANOVA) using PROC MIXED to compare the least square means (LSMeans) of a variable called lcmax across different treatments (treat) and periods. Here's a breakdown of what each part of the code does:

1. `ods trace on;`: This turns on the ODS (Output Delivery System) tracing, which allows capturing the output from various procedures.

2. `ods output LSMeans=LSMeans; ods output Diffs=Diffs; ods output Estimates=Estimates; ods output CovParms=CovParms;`: These lines direct the output from different procedures (LSMeans, Diffs, Estimates, and CovParms) to corresponding output datasets named LSMeans, Diffs, Estimates, and CovParms, respectively.

3. `PROC MIXED data=pkparm;`: This begins the PROC MIXED procedure, which is used for conducting mixed-model ANOVA. The `data=pkparm;` specifies the input dataset for the analysis.

4. `CLASS seqence subno period treat;`: This defines the categorical variables for the analysis: seqence, subno, period, and treat.

5. `MODEL lcmax = treat period / solution ddfm=satterth;`: This specifies the model to be fitted. It models the variable lcmax with treat and period as fixed effects. The `solution` option requests solutions for the fixed effects, and `ddfm=satterth` specifies the method for calculating denominator degrees of freedom.

6. `RANDOM subno(seqence);`: This specifies the random effects structure of the model. It indicates that subno is a random effect nested within seqence.

7. `LSMEANS treat / PDIFF CL alpha=0.10;`: This computes least squares means (LSMeans) for the variable treat and requests pairwise differences (`PDIFF`) between the LSMeans with confidence limits (`CL`) at a significance level of 0.10.

8. `estimate 'T/R' treat -1 1 / cl alpha=0.10;`: This estimates the ratio of geometric means between treatments T and R, with confidence limits at a significance level of 0.10.

9. `run;`: This ends the PROC MIXED procedure.

10. The subsequent part of the code performs some data manipulation. It calculates the geometric means, ratios of geometric means, and confidence intervals for the ratios.

11. Finally, there's a statement indicating the criteria for considering bioequivalence between the test (T) and reference (R) products, stating that the 90% confidence interval for the difference of the LSMeans should fall between 80.00% and 125.00%.

<u>**Project-04:**</u>
<u>**Oncology**</u>
Phase 1 Trial of Intralesional Immunotherapy with IFx-Hu2.0 Vaccine in Patients with Advanced Merkel Cell Carcinoma or Cutaneous Squamous Cell Carcinoma
Primary Objective:

- To assess the safety of vaccinating with intralesional IFx-Hu2.0 therapy in patients with Merkel cell carcinoma (MCC) or cutaneous squamous cell carcinoma (cSCC).

Primary Endpoint:

- **Safety**, defined as the absence of dose-limiting toxicities (DLTs), which is the absence of any grade 3-5, treatment-related Adverse Events (AEs) per Common Terminology Criteria for Adverse Events (CTCAE) v5.0 from the first injection (Day 1) to final follow-up (Day 28, 35, or 42 depending on dosing schedule) ± 7 days.

Safety Analysis:

- Safety analysis conducted on the safety population comprising all treated subjects.

- Safety endpoints analyzed as summary statistics during treatment or as change scores from baselines, e.g., shift tables.

- Treatment emergent adverse events (TEAEs) coded using Medical Dictionary for Regulatory Activities (MedDRA).

- Presentation of TEAE severity and relationship to study treatment by dose cohort, MedDRA system organ class (SOC), and preferred term (PT).

- Reported information for each AE includes start date, stop date, severity, relationship, outcome, and duration.

- AEs leading to premature discontinuation or serious TEAEs presented with a summary table or data listing.

- Number and percentage of subjects with treatment-related TEAEs > grade 2 per Common Terminology Criteria for Adverse Events (CTCAE) v5.0 reported by dose cohort, MedDRA SOC, and PT.

- Immune response TEAEs reported similarly.

- Summary of all TEAEs by cohort using descriptive statistics.

- Summarization of TEAE incidence by MedDRA SOC, PT, intensity, and relationship to study treatment.

- Vital Signs: Summarization of observed vital signs and changes from baseline by cohort.

- Physical Examination: Summarization of abnormal findings by dose cohort.

- Clinical Laboratory Tests: Summarization of abnormal lab values and shifts from baseline using descriptive statistics.

- ECOG: Summarization of observed ECOG performance status data.

- Other Safety Evaluations: Summarization of ECGs, imaging assessments, immune safety tests, and immunogenicity.

Exploratory Analyses:

- Descriptive reporting of exploratory laboratory correlative endpoints.

- Quantitative measurement of Emm55 expression using fresh tumor biopsy.

- Measurement of immune cell subsets in peripheral blood and biopsy samples.

- Additional immunological assessment if material permits, guided by pre-clinical work.

Project-05

Oncology

Title:

A Phase-2 Study of ENZASTAURIN in Patients with Relapsed Cutaneous T-cell Lymphoma

Primary Objective:

- To evaluate the safety and efficacy of ENZASTAURIN in patients with relapsed cutaneous T-cell lymphoma (CTCL).

Primary Endpoint: Determine the response rate using standardized criteria, including Complete Response (CR), Partial Response (PR), Stable Disease (SD), and Progressive Disease (PD).

The mSWAT score is calculated using a formula that assigns numerical values to various parameters related to skin lesions and their characteristics. These parameters typically include:

1. **Number of Patches, Plaques, or Tumors**: Each individual lesion is counted, and a score is assigned based on the total number present.

The specific formula for calculating the mSWAT score typically involves summing up the scores assigned to each parameter to obtain the overall score. However, the exact scoring system may vary depending on the specific criteria used in the assessment.

Response Categorization:

1. **Complete Response (CR):**

- Disappearance of all target lesions.

2. **Partial Response (PR):**

- At least a 30% decrease in the sum of the longest diameter of target lesions.

3. **Stable Disease (SD):**

- Neither sufficient decrease to qualify as PR nor sufficient increase to qualify as Progressive Disease (PD).

4. **Progressive Disease (PD):**

- At least a 20% increase in the sum of the longest diameter of target lesions, or the appearance of new lesions.

Sezary syndrome, an aggressive form of Cutaneous T-cell Lymphoma (CTCL), is diagnosed and monitored through the measurement of Sezary cell count, which involves the detection of malignant T-cells in the skin, blood, and lymph nodes.

To evaluate Sezary cell count, blood samples are collected from the patient, and specialized laboratory techniques are employed. Two commonly used methods for measuring the percentage of Sezary cells in the blood are lymph cytometry and flow cytometry.

In oncology, response rate, often assessed using predefined criteria like RECIST, is crucial in clinical trials. The primary statistical method used is the **Chi-square test** for comparing response rates between treatment groups or assessing proportions of responders within a single group.

***Chi-square Test Syntax**:*

PROC FREQ data=oncology_data;

*TABLES treatment_group * response_category / CHISQ;*

RUN;

This test analyzes contingency tables to determine if response rates differ significantly between groups, guiding conclusions on treatment efficacy.

PROJECT-06:

IMMUNOLOGY:

Multiple Phase 2b Studies Evaluating the Efficacy and Safety of ACTIVE DRUG for the Treatment of Participants with Moderate to Severe Psoriasis

Primary Objectives

To evaluate the dose response of JNJ-77242113 at Week 16 in participants with moderate-to-severe plaque psoriasis

Primary Endpoint

Proportion of participants achieving PASI 75 (≥75% improvement from baseline in PASI) at Week 16

Secondary Objectives:

- To evaluate the effect of JNJ-77242113 treatment on patient-reported psoriasis severity versus placebo in participants with moderate-to-severe plaque psoriasis
- Change from baseline in PASI total score at Week 16
- · Proportion of participants achieving PASI 90(≥90% improvement from baseline in PASI) at Week 16
- · Proportion of participants achieving PASI100 (100% improvement from baseline in
- PASI) at Week 16
- · Proportion of participants achieving an IGA score of cleared (0) or minimal (1) at
- Week 16
- · Proportion of participants achieving an IGA score of cleared (0) at Week 16
- · Change from baseline in BSA at Week 16
- To evaluate the effect of JNJ-77242113 treatment on patient-reported psoriasis severity versus placebo in participants with moderate-to-severe plaque psoriasis

- Frequency and type of adverse events (AEs) and serious adverse events (SAEs)
- Change from baseline in Psoriasis Symptoms and Signs Diary (PSSD) symptoms score at Week 16
- · Change from baseline in PSSD signs score at Week 16
- · Proportion of participants achieving PSSD symptoms score=0 at Week 16 among
- participants with a baseline symptom scores ≥1.
- · Proportion of participants achieving PSSD signs score=0 at Week 16 among participants with a baseline signs score ≥1.

Exploratory objectives

- To evaluate long-term clinical response of NJ77242113 treatment in participants with moderate to-severe plaque psoriasis
- Proportion of participants achieving PASI 75 (≥75% improvement in PASI from baseline of the originating study) over time through Week 36
- · Change from baseline of the originating study in PASI total score over time through
- Week 36
- · Proportion of participants achieving PASI 90 (≥90% improvement in PASI from baseline of the originating study) over time through Week 36
- · Proportion of participants achieving PASI 100 (100% improvement in PASI from baseline of the originating study) over time
- through Week 36
- · Proportion of participants achieving an IGA score of cleared (0) or minimal (1) over time through Week 36
- · Proportion of participants achieving an IGA score of cleared (0) over time through Week 36
- · Change from baseline of the originating study in body surface area (BSA) over time through Week 36
- PSSD symptoms score over CHG
- Dermatological Life Quality Index (DLQI) of 0 or 1 over time through Week 36 among participants with a baseline
- Patient-Reported Outcomes Measurement Information System29 (PROMIS-29) over time through Week 36
- PK CMAX AUC
- The incidence of anti-drug antibodies (ADAs) to JNJ-77242113
- Nail Psoriasis Area and Severity Index (NAPSI) PCHG
- Fingernail Physician's Global Assessment(fPGA)
- Physician's Global Assessment of Hands and/or Feet (hfPGA) score
- Static Physician's Global Assessment (s-PGA) of genitalia score
- Genital Psoriasis Sexual Frequency Questionnaire (GenPsSFQ) item 2 over time

What are the Efficacy variables use to achieve primary and secondary objective and endpoints?

Project-01: *COVID-19*

The primary objective is to **determine if C-Drug (AA) increases the proportion of patients** with **clinical recovery** from COVID-19symptoms on Day 14 in patients with mild to moderate COVID-19 disease compared with placebo.

Dataset Used: ADSL

Variables used:

Clinical recovery on Day 14 Flag **COVD14FL**, Clinical recovery on Day 28 Flag **COVD28FL**

Variable derivation:

If the subject met all the Clinical Recovery conditions as per SAP at Day 14 then flag as 'Y'; Else Set to 'N'

Clinical recovery on Day 14 is defined as:

- Temperature ≤ 37.7°C (oral or skin surface)
- Respiratory rate ≤ 24/minute on room air
- Shortness of breath – absent
- Cough – mild or absent on a patient-reported scale

Proportion of patients with clinical recovery of COVID-19 symptoms on Day 14 (±1 day), where clinical recovery on Day 14 is defined as:

- Temperature ≤ 37.7°C (oral or skin surface)
- Respiratory rate ≤ 24/minute on room air
- Shortness of breath – absent
- Cough – mild or absent on a patient-reported scale

A patient will be considered a clinical failure if lost to follow-up (LTFU) or hospitalized for treatment of COVID-19 disease even if the above conditions meet on Day 14.

COVD14FL	Clinical recovery on Day 14 Flag	text	200				Derived	If the subject met all the Clinical Recovery condistions as per SAP at Day 14 then flag as 'Y'; Else Set to 'N'
COVD28FL	Clinical recovery on Day 28 Flag	text	200				Derived	If the subject met all the Clinical Recovery condistions as per SAP at Day 28 then flag as 'Y'; Else Set to 'N'
COUGH14	Cough Symptom on Day 14	text	200				Derived	Set to 'Y' if FASTRESC in('MILD' 'MODERATE' 'SEVERE') else Set to 'N'
SHORT14	Shortness of breath Symptom o	text	200				Derived	Set to 'Y' if FASTRESC in('MILD' 'MODERATE' 'SEVERE') else Set to 'N'
CHILL14	Chills or shivering Symptom on	text	200				Derived	Set to 'Y' if FASTRESC in('MILD' 'MODERATE' 'SEVERE') else Set to 'N'
FEEL14	Feeling hot or feverish Symptom	text	200				Derived	Set to 'Y' if FASTRESC in('MILD' 'MODERATE' 'SEVERE') else Set to 'N'
HEAD14	Headache Symptom on Day 14	text	200				Derived	Set to 'Y' if FASTRESC in('MILD' 'MODERATE' 'SEVERE') else Set to 'N'
DIARR14	Diarrhea Symptom on Day 14	text	200				Derived	Set to 'Y' if FASTRESC not in('I DID NOT HAVE DIARRHEA AT ALL' ' ') else Set to 'N'
VOMIT14	Vomit Symptom on Day 14	text	200				Derived	Set to 'Y' if FASTRESC not in('I DID NOT VOMIT AT ALL' ' ') else Set to 'N'
TIRED14	Low energy or tiredness Sympto	text	200				Derived	Set to 'Y' if FASTRESC in('MILD' 'MODERATE' 'SEVERE') else Set to 'N'
ACHES14	Muscle or body aches Symptom	text	200				Derived	Set to 'Y' if FASTRESC in('MILD' 'MODERATE' 'SEVERE') else Set to 'N'
NASEA14	Nausea Symptom on Day 14	text	200				Derived	Set to 'Y' if FASTRESC in('MILD' 'MODERATE' 'SEVERE') else Set to 'N'
SMELL14	Smell Symptom on Day 14	text	200				Derived	Set to 'Y' if FASTRESC in('I HAVE NO SENSE OF SMELL') else Set to 'N'
TASTE14	Taste Symptom on Day 14	text	200				Derived	Set to 'Y' if FASTRESC in('I HAVE NO TASTE OF SMELL') else Set to 'N'
THROT14	Sore throat Symptom on Day 14	text	200				Derived	Set to 'Y' if FASTRESC in('MILD' 'MODERATE' 'SEVERE') else Set to 'N'
NOSE14	Stuffy or runny nose Symptom o	text	200				Derived	Set to 'Y' if FASTRESC in('MILD' 'MODERATE' 'SEVERE') else Set to 'N'
TEMP14	Temperature Symptom on Day 1	text	200				Derived	Set to 'Y' if VSSTRESN gt 37.7 else Set to 'N'
RESP14	Respiration rate Symptom on Da	text	200				Derived	Set to 'Y' if VSSTRESN gt 24 and VSTESTCD = 'RESP' else Set to 'N'

ADSL SPECIFICATION

Project-02:

Therapeutic area: cardiovascular

Primary Objective:

Assess the effect of serelaxin versus placebo on high-sensitivity cardiac troponin I (hs-cTnI) release in patients with chronic heart failure after exercise.

Primary Endpoint:

- The primary endpoint was the **analysis of efficacy variables**, including NT-proBNP, H-FABP, hs-cTnT, echocardiogram assessment, spirometry, and ergometry assessments.

Dataset used: ADBIO

Variables used:

PARAM,PARAMCD,PARAMN

```
proc ttest data=main ;
by paramn;
class trt;
var aval2 ;
ods output statistics=result2 (keep=paramn CLASS);
run;
ods trace off;
data aval1;
set result2;
if CLASS ^="Diff (1-2)";
trt=class;
run;
proc sort;by paramn trt;run;
```

Project-03:
BA/BE study
Primary Objective:

- To assess the bioequivalence of Solifenacin Succinate Tablets 10 mg from airis PHARMA Private Limited, India, with VESICARE® (Solifenacin Succinate) Tablets 10 mg from Astellas Pharma US, Inc., Northbrook, IL 60062, in healthy adult human subjects under fasting conditions.

Primary Endpoints:

- Pharmacokinetic Parameters:
- Cmax (maximum plasma concentration)
- AUC0-72 (area under the plasma concentration-time curve from time zero to 72 hours)

Dataset used: ADPK,ADPC,ADPP

> **PARAM, PARAMN, PARAMCD**
> The variable PARAM contains the description of the analysis parameter. In ADPC files, the value of PARAM represents the analyzed compound with its unit (e.g. 'Compound X (ng/mL)'); the abbreviation of the analyzed compound is stored in the variable PARAMCD. In ADPP files, the value of PARAM is the PK parameter with its unit (e.g. 'Cmax (ng/mL)'); the abbreviation of the PK parameter is stored in the variable PARAMCD. The numeric counterpart is presented in PARAMN.

Variables used:
PARAM,PARAMCD,PARAMN

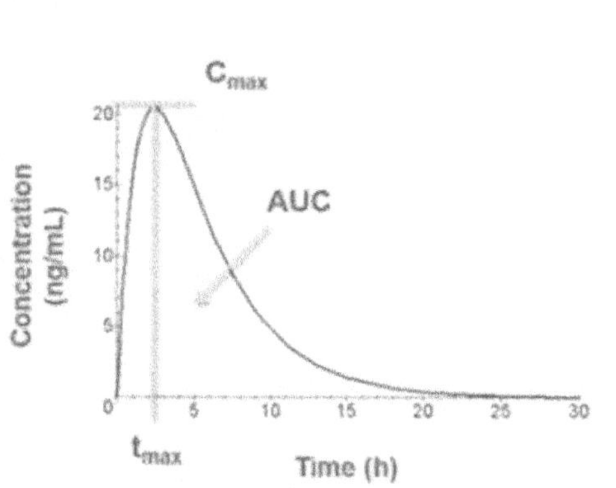

Project-04:
Oncology
Phase 1 Trial of Intralesional Immunotherapy with IFx-Hu2.0 Vaccine in Patients with Advanced Merkel Cell Carcinoma or Cutaneous Squamous Cell Carcinoma

Primary Objective:

- To assess the safety of vaccinating with intralesional IFx-Hu2.0 therapy in patients with Merkel cell carcinoma (MCC) or cutaneous squamous cell carcinoma (cSCC).

Primary Endpoint:

- **Safety**, defined as the absence of dose-limiting toxicities (DLTs), which is the absence of any grade 3-5, treatment-related Adverse Events (AEs) per Common Terminology Criteria for Adverse Events (CTCAE) v5.0 from the first injection (Day 1) to final follow-up (Day 28, 35, or 42 depending on dosing schedule) ± 7 days.

DATASEST:

All safety datasets ADAE, ADVS,ADEG,ADCM,ADMH,ADLB e.t.c

- ADSL (Analysis Data Subject-Level):This dataset contains one row per subject and includes variables that summarize subject-level data. It's often used for demographic information and baseline characteristics.
- ADLB (Analysis Data LB):ADLB datasets contain laboratory data in a standardized format for analysis. These datasets are essential for analyzing laboratory results.
- ADTTE (Analysis Data Time-to-Event):These datasets are used for time-to-event analysis, such as survival analysis. They capture information related to when specific events occur.
- ADPC (Analysis Data Pharmacokinetics Concentration):ADPC datasets are used for pharmacokinetic analysis and contain concentration-time data for drugs.
- ADAEG (Analysis Data Adverse Events General):These datasets are used to analyze adverse events data. They include information about the occurrence, severity, and timing of adverse events.
- ADQS (Analysis Data Queries):ADQS datasets contain information related to data queries and discrepancies found during data review and cleaning.
- ADTTE (Analysis Data Time-to-Event):These datasets are used for time-to-event analysis, capturing information about when specific events occur.

<u>Project-05</u>
<u>Oncology</u>
Title:
A Phase-2 Study of ENZASTAURIN in Patients with Relapsed Cutaneous T-cell Lymphoma
Primary Objective:
- To evaluate the safety and efficacy of ENZASTAURIN in patients with relapsed cutaneous T-cell lymphoma (CTCL).
Primary Endpoint: Determine the response rate using standardized criteria, including Complete Response (CR), Partial Response (PR), Stable Disease (SD), and Progressive Disease (PD).
DATASET USED:

- **Tumor Response Dataset:**This dataset documents changes in tumor size or progression using criteria like RECIST (Response Evaluation Criteria in Solid Tumors) or similar systems.
- **Progression-Free Survival (PFS) Dataset:**PFS datasets track the time patients remain free from disease progression. It's a critical endpoint in oncology trials.
- **Overall Survival (OS) Dataset**: OS datasets record the time from the start of treatment until a patient's death, a vital endpoint in oncology trials to assess long-term outcomes.
- **Objective Response Dataset**: This dataset includes information on complete and partial responses to treatment, often following RECIST criteria.
- **Biomarker Expression Dataset:**In precision medicine approaches, biomarker expression datasets capture data on the presence or levels of specific molecular markers used to guide treatment decisions.

1. **SWAT**: This could refer to a "Study Within A Trial," which is a secondary study embedded within a larger clinical trial. It could be used to explore additional endpoints or questions beyond the primary objectives of the main trial.

2. **ECOG**: This likely stands for "Eastern Cooperative Oncology Group," which is a commonly used scale to assess the functional status of cancer patients. It ranges from 0 (fully active) to 5 (dead).

3. **LESIONS**: This term generally refers to abnormal areas in tissues or organs that have been affected by disease, often used in the context of cancer to describe tumors or areas of abnormal tissue growth.

4. **IARD**: This abbreviation is not commonly used in oncology studies, but in other contexts, it could stand for "Integrated Annual Report and Data" or "Incidence, Adverse Reactions, and Deaths."

5. **EQ5D**: This likely refers to the EuroQol 5-Dimension questionnaire, a standardized instrument used to measure health-related quality of life. It assesses mobility, self-care, usual activities, pain/discomfort, and anxiety/depression.

6. **IQL/QOL**: This likely combines two terms:
- **IQL**: Possibly a typo or a specific abbreviation within the context of the study.
- **QOL**: Stands for "Quality of Life," which is an important outcome measure in oncology studies, assessing the overall well-being of patients beyond clinical endpoints.

7. **MORT**: Short for "Mortality," which refers to death, often used to analyze survival rates in oncology studies.

8. **TTEVENT**: This could mean "Time to Event," referring to the duration from the start of a treatment or intervention to the occurrence of a specific event, such as disease progression or death.

9. **BOR**: Likely stands for "Best Overall Response," which is a measure used to assess the effectiveness of cancer treatments based on tumor shrinkage or stability.

10. **PATHDY**: This abbreviation is not standard in oncology studies. It might be specific to the particular study or dataset being referenced.

11. **RESPONCE**: Likely a typo for "Response," which generally refers to the reaction of tumors to a particular treatment, often categorized as complete response, partial response, stable disease, or progressive disease.

12. **P5SQ**: This abbreviation is not standard in oncology studies. It might be specific to the particular study or dataset being referenced.

<u>PROJECT-06:</u>

IMMUNOLOGY:

Multiple Phase 2b Studies Evaluating the Efficacy and Safety of ACTIVE DRUG for the Treatment of Participants with Moderate to Severe Psoriasis

- **Primary Objectives**
- *To evaluate the dose response of JNJ-77242113 at Week 16 in participants with moderate-to-severe plaque psoriasis*
- *Primary Endpoint*
- *Proportion of participants achieving PASI 75 (≥75% improvement from baseline in PASI) at Week 16*

<u>**Immunology Efficacy Datasets:**</u>

- **ACR Response Dataset**: This dataset tracks the American College of Rheumatology (ACR) response criteria for patients in immunology trials, measuring improvements in joint tenderness and swelling, pain, and other relevant parameters.
- **CDAI (Clinical Disease Activity Index) Dataset**: CDAI is often used in trials related to autoimmune diseases like rheumatoid arthritis to assess disease activity. This dataset captures CDAI scores over time.
- **Biomarker Response Dataset**: In immunology trials, various biomarkers like cytokines or antibody levels may be measured to assess treatment efficacy. This dataset records these biomarker measurements.
- **Response Evaluation Dataset**: This dataset is crucial for assessing the response of patients to immunology treatments. It includes measurements of disease-specific indicators, such as inflammation levels, antibody titers, or specific biomarkers related to the targeted condition.
- **Clinical Disease Activity Index (CDAI) Dataset**: In trials for conditions like rheumatoid arthritis, the CDAI dataset records disease activity scores based on clinical assessments, including joint tenderness and swelling, pain, and patient global assessment.
- **American College of Rheumatology (ACR) Response Dataset**: This dataset tracks ACR response criteria, which are commonly used in immunology trials to measure improvements in disease activity. It includes variables related to joint counts, pain assessments, and other relevant parameters.
- **Biomarker Response Dataset**: In immunology trials, biomarkers like cytokines, antibodies, or specific cell counts may be measured to assess treatment efficacy. This dataset captures these biomarker measurements and their

changes over time.

- **Adverse Events Dataset:** While primarily focused on safety, the adverse events dataset may also include information on specific adverse events that can be related to the efficacy of the treatment. This dataset records the occurrence, severity, and timing of adverse events.
- **Patient-Reported Outcomes (PROs) Dataset:** In some immunology trials, PROs are used to gather data directly from patients about their symptoms and quality of life. This dataset includes patient-reported assessments of their condition and treatment-related changes.
- **Disease-Specific Endpoint Dataset:** Depending on the disease being studied, specific endpoints related to disease severity, progression, or remission may be tracked. For example, in multiple sclerosis trials, disability scores like the Expanded Disability Status Scale (EDSS) are commonly used.
- **Histopathology Dataset:** In immunology trials that involve tissue biopsies or histological assessments, this dataset records the results of histopathological examinations, including inflammation levels, tissue damage, and other relevant findings.
- **Radiographic Assessment Dataset:** In some trials, radiographic imaging is used to assess changes in disease-related features, such as joint damage in rheumatoid arthritis. This dataset includes radiographic findings and assessments.
- **Functional Assessment Dataset:** This dataset may include measurements of functional abilities relevant to the disease under study, such as the Health Assessment Questionnaire (HAQ) for rheumatoid arthritis.
- **Cardiology Efficacy Datasets:**
- **LVEF (Left Ventricular Ejection Fraction) Dataset:** This dataset is crucial in cardiology trials, especially those related to heart failure. It tracks LVEF measurements, a key indicator of cardiac function.
- **MACE (Major Adverse Cardiovascular Events) Dataset:** MACE datasets record occurrences of major adverse cardiovascular events such as myocardial infarction, stroke, or cardiovascular-related death.
- **Exercise Tolerance Dataset:** In trials for conditions like angina or heart failure, this dataset captures data on exercise tolerance and performance, often assessed through stress tests.

CHAPTER SIX

How your statistician decides the efficacy procedure?

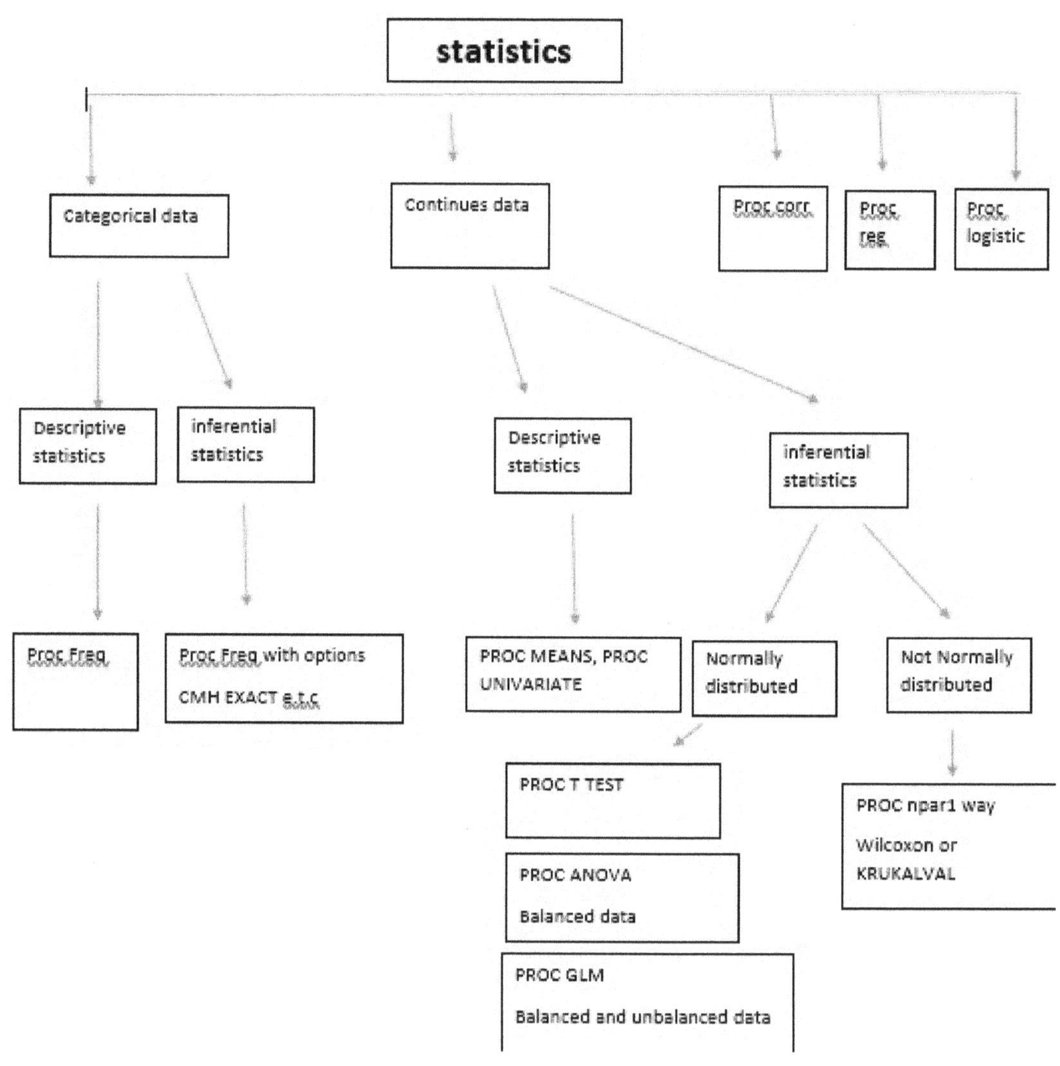

1. If a continuous variable demonstrates a normal distribution, characterized by indicators like a mean, median, and mode equal to zero, or skewness and kurtosis equal to zero, or a sample size less than 30,
2. And if a categorical variable presents with only two responses,
3. Then the recommended statistical procedure is to utilize the PROC T test.

1. If the categorical variable exhibits more than two responses,
2. Evaluate whether the data is balanced or unbalanced,
3. Opt for ANOVA (Analysis of Variance) if the data is balanced,
4. Choose GLM (General Linear Model) if the data is unbalanced.

CHAPTER SEVEN

Difference between PARAMTYPE and DTYPE

1. **Identify the Need**: Recognize that BMI needs to be derived from the collected variables height and weight.

2. **Create New Records**: For each subject and each visit, create new records where PARAMCD equals BMI.

3. **Calculate BMI**: Calculate BMI values based on the collected height and weight data.

4. **Populate PARAMTYP**: Populate PARAMTYP as DERIVED for these new records to indicate that BMI is derived from other parameters.

5. ***Populate DTYPE***: *Since the values of BMI are derived from height and weight, you need to populate DTYPE to denote the derivation method used for BMI calculation.*

So, essentially:

- Identify the need to create BMI.
- Create new records for BMI for each subject and visit.
- Calculate BMI based on height and weight.
- Populate PARAMTYP as DERIVED for these new BMI records.
- Populate DTYPE to specify the derivation method used for BMI calculation.

1. **A new row is added within a parameter with the analysis value populated based on other rows within the parameter**: In this case, you would populate DTYPE with values such as AVERAGE if the analysis value is derived from other rows within the parameter.

2. **A new row is added within a parameter with the analysis value populated based on a constant value or data from other subjects**: Similarly, for this scenario, you would populate DTYPE with a relevant value, such as AVERAGE if the analysis value is derived from constant values or data from other subjects.

3. **An analysis value (AVAL or AVALC) on an existing record is being replaced with a value based on a pre-specified algorithm**: Here, you would populate DTYPE with a value like LOCF (Last Observation Carried Forward) or WOCF (Worst Observation Carried Forward) to denote the method used for replacing the analysis value.

So, you would use DTYPE values like **AVERAGE, LOCF, or WOCF** depending on the situation described above.

PARAM	AVISIT	AVISITN	VISITNUM	VSSEQ	ABLFL	AVAL	BASE	CHG	PARAMTYP	DTYPE
Weight (kg)	Screening	-4	1	1164		99	100	.		
Weight (kg)	Run-In	-2	2	1165		101	100	.		
Weight (kg)	Baseline	0	3	1166	Y	100	100	0		
Weight (kg)	Week 24	24	4	1167		94	100	-6		
Weight (kg)	Week 48	48	5	1168		92	100	-8		
Weight (kg)	Week 52	52	6	1169		95	100	-5		
Weight (kg)	Endpoint	9999				93.5	100	-6.5		AVERAGE

PARAM	PARAMCD	AVISIT	AVISITN	VISITNUM	ABLFL	AVAL	BASE	CHG	PARAMTYP
Weight (kg)	WEIGHT	Screening	-4	1		99	100	.	
Weight (kg)	WEIGHT	Run-In	-2	2		101	100	.	
Weight (kg)	WEIGHT	Baseline	0	3	Y	100	100	0	
Weight (kg)	WEIGHT	Week 24	24	4		94	100	-6	
Weight (kg)	WEIGHT	Week 48	48	5		92	100	-8	
Weight (kg)	WEIGHT	Week 52	52	6		95	100	-5	
Log10(Weight (kg))	L10WT	Screening	-4	1		1.9956	2	.	DERIVED
Log10(Weight (kg))	L10WT	Run-In	-2	2		2.0043	2	.	DERIVED
Log10(Weight (kg))	L10WT	Baseline	0	3	Y	2	2	0	DERIVED
Log10(Weight (kg))	L10WT	Week 24	24	4		1.9731	2	-0.0269	DERIVED
Log10(Weight (kg))	L10WT	Week 48	48	5		1.9638	2	-0.0362	DERIVED
Log10(Weight (kg))	L10WT	Week 52	52	6		1.9777	2	-0.0223	DERIVED

USUBJID	TRTA	TRTAN	VSTESTCD	VISIT	VISITNUM	VSSTRESN	paramtyp
001-001	Placebo	1	HEIGHT	SCREENING	1	196	
001-001	Placebo	1	WEIGHT	SCREENING	1	116	
001-001	Placebo	1	BMI	SCREENING	1	30.19575177	DERIVED
001-001	Placebo	1	WEIGHT	WEEK 14	2	114	
001-001	Placebo	1	BMI	WEEK 14	2	29.67513536	DERIVED
001-001	Placebo	1	WEIGHT	WEEK 28	3	112	
001-001	Placebo	1	BMI	WEEK 28	3	29.15451895	DERIVED

What defines a Treatment Emergent Adverse Event (TEAE) in clinical trials, and how are they characterized?

1. **Definition of TEAE**: Treatment Emergent Adverse Events (TEAEs) are undesirable events that occur following medical treatment and were not present prior to the treatment. They can also include pre-existing events that worsen either in intensity or frequency after the treatment.

2. **Characterization of TEAEs**:

- TEAEs are events that emerge or become apparent during the course of treatment.

- These events are typically adverse in nature, meaning they are unwanted or harmful to the patient's health.

- TEAEs are distinguished from pre-existing conditions or events that were present before the initiation of treatment.

**Example: **

In a clinical trial evaluating a new medication for hypertension, suppose a patient enrolled in the study experiences dizziness for the first time after starting the medication. This dizziness would be categorized as a Treatment Emergent Adverse Event (TEAE) because it occurred following the initiation of treatment and was not present before. Similarly, if a patient's existing headache worsens in intensity after starting the medication, the **worsening** headache would also be classified as a TEAE.

USUBJID	AETERM	AEDECOD	AESOC	EPOCH	RFSTDTC ▲	AESTDTC	AEITOXGR	TRTEMFL
27899	HYPERTENSION	HYPERTENSION	VASCULAR DIS...	SCREENING	2016-06-30	2016-06-29	1	Y
27899	HYPERTENSION	HYPERTENSION	VASCULAR DIS...	TREATMENT	2016-06-30	2016-08-31	2	Y

Grades

Grade refers to the severity of the AE. The CTCAE v3.0 displays Grades 1 through 5 with unique clinical descriptions of severity for each AE based on this general guideline:

Grade 1	Mild AE
Grade 2	Moderate AE
Grade 3	Severe AE
Grade 4	Life-threatening or disabling AE
Grade 5	Death related to AE

AE data						Treatment Emergent Analysis Flag	EX data			
Unique Subject Identifier	Sequence Number	Group ID	Reported Term for the Adverse Event	Start Date/Time of Adverse Event	End Date/Time of Adverse Event		Sequence Number	Name of Treatment	Start Date/Time of Treatment	End Date/Time of Treatment
USUBJID	AESEQ	AEGRPID	AETERM	AESTDTC	AEENDTC	TRTEMFL	EXSEQ	EXTRT	EXSTDTC	EXENDTC
ABC-1001	1	1	Headache	2017-05	2017-05-11	Y	1	A	2017-05-08T08:20	2017-05
ABC-1001	2	1	Headache	2017-05-11	2017-05-22	Y	1	A	2017-05-08T08:20	2017-05
ABC-1001	3		Fever	2017-06-11	2017-06	N				
ABC-1001	4		Bone pain	2017-07	2017-08-10	Y	2	A	2017-06-15	2017-07-07
ABC-1001	4		Bone pain	2017-07	2017-08-10	Y	3	B	2017-07-21	2017-08
ABC-1001	5		Cold	2017-08-15	2017-09-13	Y	3	B	2017-07-21	2017-08
ABC-1001	5		Cold	2017-08-15	2017-09-13	Y	4	B	2017-08	2017-09-21
ABC-1001	6	2	Back pain	2017-05	2017-08-03	Y	1	A	2017-05-08T08:20	2017-05
ABC-1001	7	2	Back pain	2017-08-03		Y	3	B	2017-07-21	2017-08
ABC-1001	7	2	Back pain	2017-08-03		Y	4	B	2017-08	2017-09-21

TEAE09_SORTED

AE data							Treatment Emergent Analysis Flag	EX data			
Unique Subject Identifier	Sequence Number	Group ID	Reported Term for the Adverse Event	Severity/ Intensity	Start Date/Time of Adverse Event	End Date/Time of Adverse Event		Sequence Number	Name of Treatment	Start Date/Time of Treatment	End Date/Time of Treatment
USUBJID	AESEQ	AEGRPID	AETERM		AESTDTC	AEENDTC	TRTEMFL	EXSEQ	EXTRT	EXSTDTC	EXENDTC
ABC-1001	1	1	Headache	MODERATE	2017-05	2017-05-11	Y	1	A	2017-05-08T08:20	2017-05
ABC-1001	2	1	Headache	MILD	2017-05-11	2017-05-22	Y	1	A	2017-05-08T08:20	2017-05
ABC-1001	3		Fever	MODERATE	2017-06-11	2017-06	N				
ABC-1001	4		Bone pain	MODERATE	2017-07	2017-08-10	Y	2	A	2017-06-15	2017-07-07
ABC-1001	4		Bone pain	MODERATE	2017-07	2017-08-10	Y	3	B	2017-07-21	2017-08
ABC-1001	5		Cold	MILD	2017-08-15	2017-09-13	Y	4	B	2017-08	2017-09-21
ABC-1001	6	2	Back pain	MODERATE	2017-05	2017-08-03	Y	1	A	2017-05-08T08:20	2017-05
ABC-1001	7	2	Back pain	MILD	2017-08-03		N	4	B	2017-08	2017-09-21

How do you determine if a data set present and conditionally execute additional steps??

EXIST function is used to determine if a data set exists in the specified library. It returns a value of 1 if the data set exists and a value of 0 if the data set does not exist.

Here's the syntax for the EXIST function:

EXIST(data-set-name)

For example, if you want to check if a data set named "mydata" exists in the "work" library, you would use:

data _null_;

if exist("work.mydata") then put "Data set exists";

else put "Data set does not exist";

run;

This code will print "Data set exists" if the data set "mydata" exists in the "work" library, otherwise it will print "Data set does not exist".

```
%MACRO PC_(RELTYPE,RELTYPE1,IDVAR,FORM);
%if %sysfunc(exist(OUTDATA.PC)) %then %do;
PROC SQL;
CREATE TABLE PC_&FORM. AS
SELECT U.STUDYID,
       U.DOMAIN AS RDOMAIN,
       U.USUBJID,
       "PC&IDVAR." AS IDVAR,
       U.PC&IDVAR. AS IDVARVAL,
       "&RELTYPE." AS RELTYPE,
       T.DOMAIN AS RDOMAIN1,
       "EXSPID" AS IDVAR1,
       T.EXSPID AS IDVARVAL1,
       "&RELTYPE1." AS RELTYPE1
FROM OUTDATA.PC WHERE=(FIND(PCSPID,"&FORM.") NE 0))
INNER JOIN OUTDATA.EX(WHERE=(FIND(EXSPID,"&FORM.") N
QUIT;
%end;
%else %do;
data PC_&FORM.;
run;
%end;
%MEND;
```

CHAPTER TEN

How do you debug macros in SAS?

```
/* Debugging Macros in SAS */
  /* 1. Enable MPRINT Option: */
  options mprint;
  /* 2. Use %PUT Statements: */
  %macro mymacro(var);
  %put Variable value: &var;
  %mend mymacro;
  /* 3. Utilize %PUT and %DISPLAY Statements: */
  %macro mymacro(var);
  %put *** DEBUG: Checking variable value: &var ***;
  %if &var = 0 %then %do;
  %put *** DEBUG: Variable is zero ***;
  %end;
  %else %do;
  %put *** DEBUG: Variable is not zero ***;
  %end;
  %mend mymacro;
  /* 4. Use %PUT Statements to Track Macro Execution: */
  %macro mymacro(var);
  %put *** DEBUG: Macro started ***;
  /* Your macro code */
  %put *** DEBUG: Macro ended ***;
  %mend mymacro;
```

Debugging macros in SAS involves techniques similar to debugging regular SAS code, but with some macro-specific approaches:

1. **Enable MPRINT Option:** Setting the `options mprint;` option displays macro code generated by macro invocations. This helps track how macro variables are resolved and how macro logic is executed.

2. **Use %PUT Statements:** `%PUT` statements are invaluable for printing messages and variable values to the SAS log. Insert `%PUT` statements strategically throughout your macro code to track the values of macro variables and to verify the flow of control.

3. **Utilize %PUT and %DISPLAY Statements:** Besides `%PUT`, you can use `%DISPLAY` to print to the log with a different prefix. It's helpful for visually distinguishing debugging messages. Conditional `%PUT` statements can help in verifying specific conditions or branches of your macro logic.

4. **Use %PUT Statements to Track Macro Execution:** Insert `%PUT` statements at the beginning and end of your macro to confirm whether it's executing as expected. This provides clarity on whether the macro starts and ends as intended, especially when dealing with complex or nested macro structures.

By employing these debugging techniques, you can effectively troubleshoot and refine your SAS macros, ensuring they operate correctly and efficiently.

CHAPTER ELEVEN

How are missing dates imputed for safety analyses and missing data handled for efficacy analyses in the clinical study protocol?

Imputation of Missing Date for Safety Analyses:

- If the start time of an adverse event (AE) is missing and it occurred on the first dose day, it will be imputed as the dose time + 1 minute, and the AE will be considered a Treatment Emergent AE (TEAE).

- If the start time of an AE other than the first dose day is missing, it will be imputed as 00:01 (hh:mm).

- If the end time of an AE other than the first dose day is missing, it will be imputed as 23:59 (hh:mm).

- If the start date of any AE is missing, it will be imputed as the 1st of the month.

- If the end date of any AE is missing, it will be imputed as the last day of the month.

```
/* Imputation of Missing Date for Safety Analyses */
data safety_data;
set original_data;
/* Impute missing start time of AE */
if missing(start_time) then do;
if dose_day = 1 then start_time = dhms(date, hour, minute, 0) + 60; /* Dose time + 1 minute */
else start_time = dhms(date, 0, 1, 0); /* 00:01 (hh:mm) */
end;
/* Impute missing end time of AE */
if missing(end_time) then do;
if dose_day ne 1 then end_time = dhms(date, 23, 59, 0); /* 23:59 (hh:mm) */
end;
/* Impute missing start date of AE */
if missing(start_date) then start_date = intnx('month', date, 0, 'beginning');
/* Impute missing end date of AE */
if missing(end_date) then end_date = intnx('month', date, 0, 'end');
run;
```

USUBJID	AETERM	AESTDTC	ASTDT	ASTDTM	ASTDTF	ASTTMF
001	HEADACHE	2006-01	11JAN2006	11JAN2006:23:59:59	D	H
001	HYPOTENSION		01JAN2006	01JAN2006:23:59:59	Y	H
001	NAUSEA	2006-01-07T22:15	07JAN2006	21JAN2006:22:15:00		
001	HEADACHE	2006	01JAN2006	01JAN2006:23:59:59	M	H
001	NOSE BLEEDING	2006-01-13	13JAN2006	13JAN2006:23:59:59		H
001	EPISTAXIS	2006-01-23T22	23JAN2006	23JAN2006:22:59:59		M

CHAPTER TWELVE

How to know whether a variable exists in a dataset??

```
data sample;
input company $ count;
datalines;
cts 12
tcs 4
novartis 5
icon 7
parexel 9
roche 5
;
run;
```

	company	count
1	cts	12
2	tcs	4
3	novartis	5
4	icon	7
5	parexel	9
6	roche	5

```
data _null_;
dsid=open('sample');
check=varnum(dsid,'Company');
if check=0 then put 'Variable does not exist';
else put 'Variable is located in column ' check +(_1) '.';
run;
```

```
84
85    data _null_;
86       dsid=open('sample');
87       check=varnum(dsid,'Company');
88       if check=0 then put 'Variable does not exist';
89       else put 'Variable is located in column ' check +(_1) '.';
90    run;

NOTE: Variable _1 is uninitialized.
Variable is located in column 1
NOTE: DATA statement used (Total process time):
      real time         0.00 seconds
      cpu time          0.00 seconds
```

- **VARNUM**: Variable number, represents position of variables in a dataset.
- **DSID**: Dataset identifier, identifies an open dataset in SAS.

CHAPTER THIRTEEN

In a clinical trial for a new medication, what are Type I and Type II errors, and how do they influence the interpretation of the results?

In statistics, Type I and Type II errors are two types of errors that can occur when testing hypotheses.

1. **Type I Error (False Positive):** This error occurs when we reject a true null hypothesis. In other words, we conclude that there is a significant effect or difference when there isn't one in reality. The probability of committing a Type I error is denoted by α (alpha), hence it's also called the alpha error. It represents the level of significance in hypothesis testing.

Example: Let's say we are testing a new drug's effectiveness. The null hypothesis (H0) is that the drug has no effect, but in reality, it does not cause any harm either. However, due to random chance or other factors, our test might incorrectly lead us to reject the null hypothesis and conclude that the drug is effective when it's actually not.

2. **Type II Error (False Negative):** This error occurs when we fail to reject a false null hypothesis. In other words, we conclude that there is no significant effect or difference when there actually is one. The probability of committing a Type II error is denoted by β (beta).

Example: Continuing with the drug example, let's say the drug does have a significant effect in treating a disease. However, due to limited sample size or other factors, our test might fail to detect this effect, leading us to accept the null hypothesis that the drug is ineffective.

Both Type I and Type II errors are crucial considerations in hypothesis testing because they impact the validity of our conclusions. The balance between these two types of errors often depends on factors such as sample size, effect size, and the chosen level of significance (α).

	Null Hypothesis is TRUE	Null Hypothesis is FALSE
Reject null hypothesis	Type I Error (False positive)	Correct Outcome! (True positive)
Fail to reject null hypothesis	Correct Outcome! (True negative)	Type II Error (False negative)

CHAPTER FOURTEEN

Could you explain how RECIST (Response Evaluation Criteria in Solid Tumors) is utilized in clinical SAS programming within oncology, providing example

RECIST (Response Evaluation Criteria in Solid Tumors) is a set of guidelines used in oncology clinical trials to assess tumor response to treatment. These criteria provide standardized methods for measuring tumor size and determining whether a patient's tumor is responding, stable, or progressing during the course of treatment. In clinical SAS programming in oncology, RECIST guidelines are often implemented to analyze and report tumor response data.

Here's how RECIST works with examples:

1. **Baseline Assessment:**

- Before starting treatment, the baseline tumor measurements are recorded using imaging techniques like CT scans or MRIs.

- Example: A patient's baseline CT scan shows a lung tumor with a longest diameter of 3 cm.

2. **Response Evaluation:**

- After treatment initiation, subsequent imaging scans are performed at regular intervals (e.g., every 6 weeks) to assess tumor response based on RECIST criteria.

- Tumor response is categorized into four main types:

- **Complete Response (CR):** Disappearance of all target lesions.

- **Partial Response (PR):** At least a 30% decrease in the sum of the longest diameters of target lesions.

- **Stable Disease (SD):** Neither sufficient shrinkage to qualify for PR nor sufficient increase to qualify for Progressive Disease (PD).

- **Progressive Disease (PD):** At least a 20% increase in the sum of the longest diameters of target lesions or the appearance of new lesions.

- Example: After 6 weeks of treatment, the follow-up CT scan shows that the lung tumor has shrunk to a longest diameter of 2 cm, indicating a partial response according to RECIST.

3. **Reporting and Analysis:**

- In clinical SAS programming, the tumor response data collected according to RECIST criteria are analyzed and summarized.

- This involves calculating response rates, duration of response, progression-free survival, and other relevant endpoints for further statistical analysis.

- Example: Using SAS, a programmer might generate tables and figures to present the distribution of response categories, time-to-event analyses, and other relevant statistics for clinical trial reports.

CHAPTER FIFTEEN

Analysis Date Analysis Study Day

In clinical research, "Analysis Date" and "Analysis Study Day" are important concepts used to track and analyze data over time. Here's what they typically refer to:

1. **Analysis Date:**

- The Analysis Date is the specific date on which data analysis is performed.

- It marks the point in time when the analysis is conducted and the results are generated.

- This date is often recorded as a reference point for interpreting the results of the analysis.

- In clinical trials, the analysis date might coincide with the completion of data collection for a particular phase or time point.

2. **Analysis Study Day:**

- The Analysis Study Day refers to the number of days from a reference point (e.g., the start of the study) to the Analysis Date.

- It is a standardized way of expressing time-related information in clinical research, especially in longitudinal studies.

- Analysis Study Day allows researchers to track changes or events over time relative to the start of the study.

- For example, if a study has been ongoing for 100 days and the Analysis Date is on the 50th day of the study, the Analysis Study Day for that date would be 50.

Both Analysis Date and Analysis Study Day are crucial for interpreting and contextualizing data in clinical research, providing insights into the progression of events and outcomes over time.

USUBJID	LBDTC	LBTEST	TRTSDT	ADT	ADY
765/15-001-S1	2016-11-08	Cholesterol	07NOV2016	08NOV2016	2
765/15-001-S1	2016-12-16	Cholesterol	07NOV2016	16DEC2016	40
765/15-001-S2	2016-11-08	Cholesterol	09NOV2016	08NOV2016	-1
765/15-001-S2	2016-12-16	Cholesterol	09NOV2016	16DEC2016	38
765/15-001-S3	2016-11-	Cholesterol	09NOV2016	01NOV2016	-8

```
DATA TEST1;
SET TEST;
format ADT date9. ADY 8.;
 if length(LBDTC) >= 10 then
ADT = mdy(substr(LBDTC,6,2), substr(LBDTC,9,2), substr(LBDTC,1,4));

  ELSE if length(LBDTC) >= 8 then
ADT = mdy(substr(LBDTC,6,2), "01", substr(LBDTC,1,4));

if ADT NE . and TRTSDT NE . then do;

if ADT LT TRTSDT then ADY = ADT - TRTSDT;
else                 ADY = ADT - TRTSDT + 1;
end;
RUN;
```

CHAPTER SIXTEEN

Can you summarize Dose Limiting Toxicities (DLT) in clinical trials, including their definition, significance, and assessment methods? Please provide

Dose Limiting Toxicities (DLT) are adverse events or side effects of a treatment that are considered serious enough to limit the dosage that can be safely administered to patients in a clinical trial. These toxicities are typically defined prior to the start of the trial and serve as important safety endpoints.

Example:

Let's consider a hypothetical clinical trial testing a new chemotherapy drug for the treatment of lung cancer. The trial protocol may specify that any patient who experiences severe nausea and vomiting requiring hospitalization within the first two cycles of treatment will be considered to have experienced a dose-limiting toxicity. If a predefined number or percentage of patients in a particular dose cohort experience this toxicity, it may trigger a dose adjustment or even discontinuation of that dose level.

Primary and Secondary Objectives:

- **Primary Objective:** The primary objective of a clinical trial involving DLTs may be to determine the maximum tolerated dose (MTD) of the investigational drug. This is the highest dose level at which a specific percentage of patients do not experience DLTs.

- **Secondary Objectives:** Secondary objectives may include assessing the safety profile of the drug, evaluating its efficacy, and exploring pharmacokinetics or pharmacodynamics.

**SAS Code with PROCEDURE: **

Below is a simplified example of SAS code using the PROCEDURE statement to analyze dose-limiting toxicities in a clinical trial dataset. This code assumes a dataset named "trial_data" containing information about adverse events and dose levels.

```
/* Define dataset and variables */
data trial_data;
input patient_id dose_level toxicity $;
datalines;
1 1 None
2 1 None
3 1 Severe nausea
4 2 None
5 2 Severe vomiting
6 3 None
7 3 None
8 3 Severe diarrhea
```

```
9 3 None
10 3 None
;
run;
/* Define DLT criteria */
%let dlt_criteria = Severe nausea Severe Vomiting Severe diarrhea;
/* Create binary variable indicating DLT */
data trial_data;
set trial_data;
if toxicity in (&dlt_criteria) then dlt = 1;
else dlt = 0;
run;
/* Calculate proportion of patients experiencing DLT at each dose level */
proc freq data=trial_data;
tables dose_level*dlt / out=dlt_summary;
run;
/* Identify dose level with MTD */
proc sql;
select dose_level, sum(dlt) as num_dlt
from dlt_summary
where dose_level ne 0
group by dose_level
having num_dlt = 0;
quit;
```

In this SAS code:

- We first define the dataset containing patient data.

- We then define the criteria for DLTs using a macro variable.

- Next, we create a binary variable indicating whether each adverse event meets the DLT criteria.

- We use PROC FREQ to calculate the proportion of patients experiencing DLT at each dose level.

- Finally, we use PROC SQL to identify the dose level at which no patients experienced a DLT, which would be considered the MTD.

CHAPTER SEVENTEEN

What are the differences between PROC MEANS, PROC UNIVARIATE, and PROC SUMMARY in SAS?

- **PROC MEANS**: PROC MEANS calculates basic descriptive statistics such as mean, median, minimum, maximum, and standard deviation for numeric variables in a dataset. It provides summary statistics for each variable specified in the VAR statement, optionally grouped by variables specified in the BY statement. PROC MEANS is primarily used for quick summaries of numeric data.

- **PROC UNIVARIATE**: PROC UNIVARIATE provides comprehensive univariate statistics for one or more variables, including measures of location (mean, median), spread (standard deviation, range), shape (skewness, kurtosis), and distribution (percentiles, histograms). It also performs tests for normality and outliers detection. PROC UNIVARIATE offers more detailed analysis compared to PROC MEANS.

- **PROC SUMMARY**: PROC SUMMARY is a versatile procedure for summarizing data. It can calculate a wide range of statistics, similar to PROC MEANS and PROC UNIVARIATE, but with greater flexibility. PROC SUMMARY allows you to specify the statistics you want to compute using various statements and options. It also supports both simple and complex summarization tasks, such as creating customized summary statistics or calculating multiple statistics for different subgroups.

In summary, while all three procedures can generate summary statistics, PROC MEANS is the simplest and most commonly used for basic summaries, PROC UNIVARIATE provides more comprehensive univariate statistics and distribution analysis, and PROC SUMMARY offers greater flexibility and customization options for summarizing data. The choice of procedure depends on the specific analysis requirements and the level of detail needed in the summary statistics.

CHAPTER EIGHTEEN

What is ODS in SAS, and how is it used to control output formatting and destination?

ODS (Output Delivery System) in SAS is a powerful feature that allows users to control the output formatting and destination of SAS output. With ODS, users can direct output to various destinations such as HTML, PDF, RTF, Excel, and more, enabling flexible reporting options.

Additionally, ODS enables customization of output appearance, including fonts, colors, titles, footnotes, and layout. This functionality streamlines the process of generating professional-looking reports and facilitates sharing of results in different formats.

SAS Code Example:

/* Example of using ODS to create a PDF report */
ods pdf file='output.pdf';
proc print data=mydataset;
run;
ods pdf close;

```
ODS ESCAPECHAR='^';
OPTIONS ORIENTATION= LANDSCAPE;
ODS RTF FILE ="G:\COVID13_102023\OUTPUTS\LIS2.RTF"
STYLE=styles.test;
```

In this example:

- `ods pdf file='output.pdf';` *sets the destination to a PDF file named "output.pdf".*

- `proc print data=mydataset;` *is an example of a SAS procedure used to print the contents of the dataset "mydataset".*

- `ods pdf close;` *closes the PDF destination, finalizing the report.*

CHAPTER NINETEEN

What are the differences in regulatory submissions for clinical trial drug approvals between the US Food and Drug Administration (FDA) and the EMA

Regulatory submissions for clinical trial drug approvals to the FDA and EMA exhibit several distinctions:

1. **Application Types:**
- The FDA typically receives Investigational New Drug (IND) applications for initiating clinical trials in the US.
- The EMA accepts Clinical Trial Applications (CTAs) for conducting trials within the European Union.

2. **Regulatory Processes:**
- The FDA follows a phased approach in clinical trial evaluation, starting with Phase 1 trials and progressing to Phase 2 and Phase 3.
- The EMA may conduct a concurrent review of multiple trial phases, allowing for more streamlined evaluations.

3. **Regulatory Guidance:**
- The FDA provides detailed guidance documents and regulations for clinical trial design, conduct, and reporting.
- The EMA offers similar guidance documents tailored to European regulatory standards.

4. **Data Requirements:**
- Both agencies require comprehensive preclinical and clinical data to support drug approval.
- The FDA emphasizes adherence to Good Clinical Practice (GCP) standards, while the EMA follows the International Conference on Harmonisation (ICH) guidelines.

5. **Geographical Reach:**
- FDA approvals grant access to the US market, while EMA approvals facilitate market access across the European Union.

6. **Approval Timelines:**
- Approval timelines may vary between the FDA and EMA, influenced by factors such as submission completeness, review workload, and agency priorities.

In summary, while both the FDA and EMA aim to ensure the safety and efficacy of clinical trial drugs, differences in application types, regulatory processes, and geographical scope necessitate tailored approaches for submissions to each agency.

CHAPTER TWENTY

What is the role of DATA _NULL_ in SAS clinical programming?

In SAS clinical programming, DATA _NULL_ is a useful technique for performing tasks that do not involve creating an actual SAS dataset. Instead, it allows users to generate output or execute procedures without storing data. Some common uses of DATA _NULL_ in SAS clinical programming include:

1. **Generating Custom Reports:** DATA _NULL_ can be used to create custom reports or listings by using PUT statements to write text or variable values to the SAS log or an external file.

2. **Performing Calculations:** It can be used to perform calculations or data manipulations without the need to store intermediate or final results in a dataset.

3. **Executing Macro Programs:** DATA _NULL_ can execute macro programs, making it useful for automating repetitive tasks or generating dynamic code.

4. **Control Statements:** It can be used in conjunction with conditional logic or looping statements to control program flow or perform iterative processes.

Overall, DATA _NULL_ provides flexibility and efficiency in SAS clinical programming by allowing users to perform tasks that do not require the creation of a physical dataset, thereby conserving memory and storage resources.

CHAPTER TWENTY-ONE

What is PROC LIFETEST in SAS clinical analysis, and how is it utilized?

PROC LIFETEST is a SAS procedure commonly used in clinical analysis for survival data. It is designed to analyze time-to-event data, such as time until death or time until recurrence of a disease. PROC LIFETEST provides various statistical methods for estimating survival functions, comparing survival curves between groups, and testing for differences in survival times.

Key functionalities of PROC LIFETEST include:

1. Kaplan-Meier Estimation: PROC LIFETEST can estimate the survival function using the Kaplan-Meier method, which is a nonparametric approach that accounts for censored observations.

2. Comparing Survival Curves: It enables comparison of survival curves between different groups using methods like the log-rank test, Wilcoxon test, or Gehan-Breslow test.

3. Stratified Analysis: PROC LIFETEST allows for stratified analysis to examine survival differences while controlling for other variables.

4. Censoring Handling: It handles censored observations effectively, accounting for in4dividuals who have not experienced the event of interest by the end of the study period.

5. Graphical Output: PROC LIFETEST produces graphical output, including Kaplan-Meier survival curves and corresponding log-rank test statistics.

Example with SAS Code:

/ Example of using PROC LIFETEST to compare survival curves */*
proc lifetest data=mydata;
*time survival_time*status(1);*
strata treatment_group;
logrank test;
run;

In this example:

- `data=mydata` specifies the input dataset containing survival data.

- `time survival_time*status(1);` specifies the time-to-event variable (survival_time) and the censoring variable (status). The value "1" indicates the event of interest (e.g., death).

- `strata treatment_group;` stratifies the analysis by the treatment group variable.

- `logrank test;` performs the log-rank test to compare survival curves between treatment groups.

This PROC LIFETEST code would generate output including Kaplan-Meier survival curves for each treatment group and the corresponding log-rank test statistic to assess differences in survival times between groups.

CHAPTER TWENTY-TWO

What are some standard operating procedures (SOPs) commonly followed in Clinical Research Organizations (CROs) for clinical statistics

1. **Protocol Review and Development:**
   - SOPs for reviewing and developing study protocols to ensure statistical considerations are appropriately addressed.
   - Guidelines for sample size determination, randomization procedures, and statistical analysis plans (SAPs).

2. **Statistical Analysis Plan (SAP) Development:**
   - Procedures for creating SAPs outlining the statistical methods, endpoints, and analysis techniques for clinical trials.
   - SOPs for review and approval of SAPs by relevant stakeholders, including sponsors and regulatory authorities.

3. **Data Management and Quality Control:**
   - SOPs for data collection, management, and cleaning processes to ensure data integrity and quality.
   - Procedures for database lock, data reconciliation, and handling of missing or incomplete data.

4. **Randomization and Blinding:**
   - Guidelines for implementing randomization procedures and maintaining treatment blinding to minimize bias.
   - SOPs for generating randomization schedules, assigning treatment allocations, and ensuring blinding integrity.

5. **Statistical Analysis and Reporting:**
   - SOPs for conducting statistical analyses according to predefined SAPs, including primary and secondary endpoints.
   - Procedures for generating statistical outputs, tables, listings, and figures for clinical study reports (CSRs) and regulatory submissions.

6. **Interim Analysis and Data Monitoring:**
   - Guidelines for conducting interim analyses and interim data monitoring to assess safety and efficacy endpoints.
   - SOPs for data monitoring committees (DMCs) and adaptive trial design methodologies.

7. **Quality Assurance and Regulatory Compliance:**
   - Procedures for ensuring compliance with regulatory requirements, Good Clinical Practice (GCP) guidelines, and industry standards.
   - SOPs for internal audits, quality control checks, and documentation of deviations or protocol amendments.

8. **Training and Development:**
   - SOPs for training clinical statisticians on relevant statistical methods, software tools, and regulatory guidelines.
   - Guidelines for ongoing professional development and knowledge sharing within the statistical team.

9. **Collaboration with Other Functional Areas:**

- Procedures for collaboration with other functional areas within the CRO, including clinical operations, data management, and regulatory affairs.

- SOPs for effective communication and coordination to ensure smooth conduct of clinical trials.

10. **Continuous Improvement and Process Optimization:**

- SOPs for evaluating and improving statistical processes, methodologies, and tools based on lessons learned and industry best practices.

- Guidelines for implementing process optimizations and quality improvement initiatives to enhance efficiency and effectiveness.

CHAPTER TWENTY-THREE

How can BDS datasets be created in ADaM IG using SAS programming?

1. **Review ADaM IG Specifications:**
   - Familiarize yourself with the specifications and requirements outlined in the ADaM IG document.
   2. **Data Preparation:**
   - Prepare the source data in a format suitable for analysis.
   - Perform data cleaning and transformation.
   3. **Create BDS Datasets:**
   - Use SAS programming to create BDS datasets based on ADaM IG specifications.
   - Define variables, formats, and attributes.

```
/* Example: Creating BDS dataset using DATA step */
data bds_dataset;
/* Define variables */
length variable1 $20 variable2 8;
format variable2 date9.;
/* Data statements */
input variable1 variable2;
datalines;
/* Input data */
value1 date1
value2 date2
/* More data lines */
;
run;
```

4. **Variable Mapping and Derivation:**
   - Map variables from source data to corresponding variables in BDS datasets.
   - Perform variable derivations as necessary.

```
/* Example: Mapping and derivation */
data bds_dataset;
set source_data;
/* Map variables */
variable1_new = source_variable1;
/* Perform derivation */
variable2_new = variable2 * 2;
run;
```

5. **Data Validation:**
   - Validate BDS datasets for accuracy and completeness.
   - Check for missing values, outliers, and inconsistencies.

6. **Metadata Documentation:**
- Document metadata for BDS datasets.

```
/* Example: Metadata documentation */
proc datasets library=mylib nolist;
modify bds_dataset;
label variable1_new = 'Description of variable1_new';
format variable2_new date9.;
run;
```

7. **Review and Validation:**
- Review BDS datasets with stakeholders.
- Validate datasets against ADaM IG specifications.

8. **Submission Package Preparation:**
- Prepare BDS datasets as part of submission package for regulatory authorities.

9. **Version Control and Documentation:**
- Maintain version control for BDS datasets.
- Document deviations from ADaM IG specifications.

CHAPTER TWENTY-FOUR

What is a scatter plot, and how is it utilized in data analysis?

A scatter plot is a graphical representation used to visualize the relationship between two continuous variables in a dataset. Each point on the plot represents a single observation, with its position determined by the values of the two variables being compared. Scatter plots are commonly used to identify patterns, trends, correlations, or outliers in the data.

Key features of scatter plots include:

1. **X and Y Axes:** The two axes represent the values of the two variables being compared. The independent variable is typically plotted on the X-axis, while the dependent variable is plotted on the Y-axis.

2. **Data Points:** Each data point on the plot represents a single observation or data pair, with its position determined by the values of the two variables.

3. **Trend Line:** In some cases, a trend line or regression line may be added to the plot to visually represent the overall trend or relationship between the variables.

4. **Correlation:** The clustering and direction of the data points on the plot can provide insights into the strength and direction of the relationship between the variables. Positive correlation is indicated by data points moving upward from left to right, while negative correlation is indicated by data points moving downward.

5. **Outliers:** Outliers, or data points that deviate significantly from the overall pattern of the data, can be identified visually on the scatter plot. These outliers may warrant further investigation to determine their cause or significance.

Overall, scatter plots are valuable tools in data analysis for exploring relationships between variables, identifying patterns or trends, and detecting outliers or unusual observations in the data.

Example with SAS Code:

```
/* Example of creating a scatter plot in SAS */
proc sgplot data=mydata;
scatter x=variable1 y=variable2 / markerattrs=(color=blue);
xaxis label="Variable 1";
yaxis label="Variable 2";
run;
```

In this example:

- `proc sgplot` initiates the procedure for creating statistical graphics in SAS.

- `scatter` specifies the type of plot (scatter plot).

- `x=variable1 y=variable2` indicates the variables to be plotted on the X and Y axes, respectively.

- `markerattrs=(color=blue)` sets the color of the markers (data points) on the plot.

- `xaxis` and `yaxis` statements label the X and Y axes, respectively.

This SAS code would generate a scatter plot with variable1 on the X-axis and variable2 on the Y-axis, using blue markers to represent the data points.

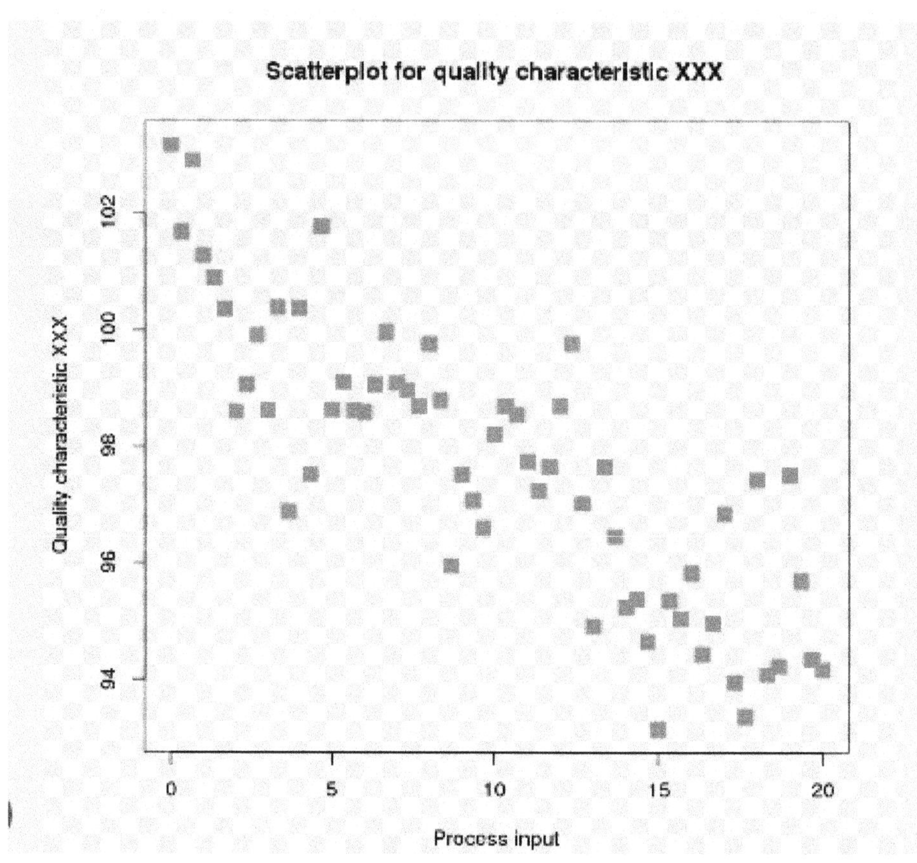

Scatterplot for quality characteristic XXX
Quality characteristic XXX
Process input

CHAPTER TWENTY-FIVE

Lab shift table

In clinical SAS, a "shift table" typically refers to a tabular representation of shifts or changes in laboratory values or parameters observed over time, treatment groups, or other relevant factors within a clinical study or research project.

Here's how a shift table might be structured and used in a clinical SAS analysis:

1. **Structure**:

- The table typically consists of rows and columns, with each row representing a specific laboratory parameter or biomarker, and each column representing different time points, treatment groups, or other categories of interest.

- The values within the table cells indicate the magnitude and direction of the shift or change in the laboratory parameter from one time point or category to another.

2. **Usage**:

- Shift tables are commonly used in clinical data analysis to summarize and visualize changes in laboratory values over the course of a study.

- They help researchers and clinicians identify trends, patterns, and differences in treatment effects, disease progression, or adverse events across different study groups or time periods.

- Shift tables can be included in clinical study reports, regulatory submissions, or presentations to stakeholders for data interpretation and decision-making.

3. **Example**:

- An example of a shift table might display laboratory parameters such as blood pressure, cholesterol levels, or biomarker concentrations at baseline and various follow-up time points for different treatment arms in a clinical trial.

- Each cell in the table could show the mean or median change in the parameter value from baseline to the respective time point, along with statistical measures of variability or significance.

In summary, a shift table in clinical SAS is a valuable tool for summarizing and analyzing changes in laboratory parameters over time or across different study groups, providing insights into treatment effects and disease progression.

	USUBJID	AVISIT	PARCAT	PARAM	LBORRES	LBORNRLO	LBORNRHI	LBNRIND	ABLFL	SHIFT1
1	765/15-001-S1	Screening	HEMATOLOGY	Monocytes/Leukocytes(%)	4	5.6	14.8	LOW	Y	LOW
2	765/15-001-S1	Treatment Period 1	HEMATOLOGY	Monocytes/Leukocytes(%)	6.6	5.6	14.8	NORMAL		LOW
3	765/15-001-S1	Treatment Period 2	HEMATOLOGY	Monocytes/Leukocytes(%)	6.6	5.6	14.8	NORMAL		LOW
4	765/15-001-S1	End of Treatment	HEMATOLOGY	Monocytes/Leukocytes(%)	6.6	5.6	14.8	NORMAL		LOW
5	765/15-001-S2	Screening	HEMATOLOGY	Monocytes/Leukocytes(%)	5.6	5.6	14.8	NORMAL	Y	NORMAL
6	765/15-001-S2	Treatment Period 1	HEMATOLOGY	Monocytes/Leukocytes(%)	5.2	5.6	14.8	LOW		NORMAL
7	765/15-001-S2	Treatment Period 2	HEMATOLOGY	Monocytes/Leukocytes(%)	5.2	5.6	14.8	LOW		NORMAL
8	765/15-001-S2	End of Treatment	HEMATOLOGY	Monocytes/Leukocytes(%)	5.2	5.6	14.8	LOW		NORMAL
9	765/15-001-S3	Screening	HEMATOLOGY	Monocytes/Leukocytes(%)	62.9	5.6	14.8	HIGH	Y	HIGH
10	765/15-001-S3	Treatment Period 1	HEMATOLOGY	Monocytes/Leukocytes(%)	4.5	5.6	14.8	LOW		HIGH
11	765/15-001-S3	Treatment Period 2	HEMATOLOGY	Monocytes/Leukocytes(%)	4.5	5.6	14.8	LOW		HIGH
12	765/15-001-S3	End of Treatment	HEMATOLOGY	Monocytes/Leukocytes(%)	4.5	5.6	14.8	LOW		HIGH
13	765/15-001-S4	Screening	HEMATOLOGY	Monocytes/Leukocytes(%)	5.8	5.6	14.8	NORMAL	Y	NORMAL
14	765/15-001-S4	Treatment Period 1	HEMATOLOGY	Monocytes/Leukocytes(%)	4.6	5.6	14.8	LOW		NORMAL
15	765/15-001-S4	Treatment Period 2	HEMATOLOGY	Monocytes/Leukocytes(%)	4.6	5.6	14.8	LOW		NORMAL
16	765/15-001-S4	End of Treatment	HEMATOLOGY	Monocytes/Leukocytes(%)	4.6	5.6	14.8	LOW		NORMAL
17	765/15-001-S5	Screening	HEMATOLOGY	Monocytes/Leukocytes(%)	6.6	5.6	14.8	NORMAL	Y	NORMAL
18	765/15-001-S5	Treatment Period 1	HEMATOLOGY	Monocytes/Leukocytes(%)	4.6	5.6	14.8	LOW		NORMAL
19	765/15-001-S5	Treatment Period 2	HEMATOLOGY	Monocytes/Leukocytes(%)	4.6	5.6	14.8	LOW		NORMAL
20	765/15-001-S5	End of Treatment	HEMATOLOGY	Monocytes/Leukocytes(%)	4.6	5.6	14.8	LOW		NORMAL

LBORRES : Result or Finding in Original Units
LBORNRLO: Reference Range Lower Limit in Orig Unit
LBORNRHI :Reference Range Upper Limit in Orig Unit
LBNRIND :Reference Range Indicator

	PARCAT	PARAM	SHIFT1	LOW	NORMAL
1	HEMATOLOGY	Monocytes/Leukocytes(%)	HIGH	1	
2	HEMATOLOGY	Monocytes/Leukocytes(%)	LOW		1
3	HEMATOLOGY	Monocytes/Leukocytes(%)	NORMAL	3	

```
PROC TRANSPOSE DATA=COUNT OUT=FINAL;
BY PARCAT  PARAM SHIFT1;
ID LBNRIND;
VAR COUNT;
RUN;
```

Table1 :   Shift Table from Baseline to End of treatment

Parameter category	Parameter (Unit)	Baseline	End of Treatment (N=5)		
			LOW	NORMAL	HIGH
HEMATOLOGY	Monocytes/Leukocytes(%)	LOW	0	1(20.0)	0
		NORMAL	3(60.0)	0	0
		HIGH	1(20.0)	0	0

How can you ensure consistency of units for the same parameter in ADaM datasets derived from LAB data using SAS programming?

To ensure consistency of units for the same parameter in ADaM datasets derived from LAB data using SAS programming, you can follow these steps:

1. **Standardize Units during Data Transformation: **

- Apply appropriate conversions or transformations to ensure that units are standardized across different datasets.

- Use SAS programming code to perform unit conversions if necessary.

2. **Compare Units across Datasets:**

- Write SAS code to compare units for the same parameter across different datasets.

- Identify any inconsistencies in units and address them accordingly.

3. **Document Units in Metadata:**

- Document units of measurement for each variable in the ADaM datasets using metadata.

- Include this information in data definition documentation or data dictionaries.

4. **Implement Data Review Checks:**

- Develop SAS programs to perform data review checks specifically targeting unit consistency.

- Compare units between LAB data and corresponding variables in ADaM datasets.

Here's an example of how you can use SAS programming code to perform unit consistency checks:

```
/* Step 1: Convert units if necessary */
/* Example: Convert mg/dL to mmol/L for glucose variable */
data adamlab;
set labdata;
if labtest = 'Glucose' then glucose_mmol = glucose_mgdl / 18.0159;
/* Other variable conversions can be performed similarly */
run;
/* Step 2: Compare units across datasets */
/* Example: Check consistency of units for glucose variable */
proc sql;
select distinct unit
from labdata;
quit;
proc sql;
select distinct unit
from adamlab
```

where labtest = 'Glucose';
quit;
/ Step 3: Document units in metadata */*
/ Example: Include unit information in dataset metadata */*
proc datasets library=work nolist;
modify adamlab;
attrib glucose_mmol label='Glucose (mmol/L)' format=best.;
/ Other variable metadata can be modified similarly */*
quit;
/ Step 4: Implement data review checks */*
/ Example: Compare units between LAB data and ADaM dataset */*
proc compare base=labdata compare=adamlab;
id patient_id labtest;
var glucose glucose_mmol;
run;

In this example:

- Step 1 performs any necessary unit conversions using SAS data step programming.

- Step 2 checks the consistency of units across datasets using SQL procedures.

- Step 3 modifies dataset metadata to document units of measurement.

- Step 4 compares units between LAB data and the corresponding variables in ADaM datasets using PROC COMPARE.

By incorporating these steps into your SAS programming workflow, you can ensure consistency of units for the same parameter in ADaM datasets derived from LAB data.

CHAPTER TWENTY-SEVEN

Why is imputation important in clinical data analysis, and what are its specific implications in clinical SAS projects

1. **Necessity of Imputation**: Imputation is crucial in clinical data analysis to handle missing values effectively, ensuring that the analysis accurately reflects the available data and provides meaningful insights.

2. **Impact of Missing Data**: Missing data can lead to biased results and loss of statistical power in clinical trials, impacting the reliability and validity of study findings.

3. **Preservation of Dataset Integrity**: Imputation helps preserve the integrity of the dataset by filling in missing values, thereby allowing researchers to maintain a sufficient sample size and reduce potential bias introduced by incomplete cases.

4. **Role in Safety Analyses**: In safety analyses of clinical trials, imputation is essential for ensuring that all safety-related data points, such as adverse event dates and times, are accounted for. This enables comprehensive evaluation of treatment safety profiles over time.

5. **Adherence to Protocol Guidelines**: Handling missing data in efficacy analyses according to predefined protocol guidelines ensures transparency and adherence to study protocols. This approach maintains the validity of treatment outcomes and supports informed decision-making in clinical research and healthcare settings.

CHAPTER TWENTY-EIGHT

What are population flags in ADaM (Analysis Data Model) for clinical SAS projects, and how are they utilized?

1. **Definition of Population Flags:**

- Population flags categorize subjects into various analysis populations, including but not limited to Intent-to-Treat (ITT), Per Protocol (PP), and Safety populations.

- They indicate whether subjects meet specific criteria for inclusion in each analysis population, providing a structured approach to data analysis.

2. **Types of Population Flags:**

- **Intent-to-Treat (ITT):** Includes all randomized subjects, regardless of protocol deviations or non-compliance with treatment.

- **Per Protocol (PP):** Includes subjects who strictly adhere to the protocol criteria, excluding those with major protocol violations.

- **Safety Population:** Includes all subjects who receive at least one dose of the investigational product, typically used for safety analyses.

- **Efficacy Population:** Includes subjects who meet specific criteria for assessing treatment efficacy, often defined based on protocol-specified endpoints.

- **Modified ITT (mITT):** Similar to ITT but may exclude certain subjects with major protocol deviations that could impact efficacy assessments.

- **As-Treated Population:** Includes subjects according to the actual treatment received, regardless of protocol assignment.

- **On-Treatment Population:** Includes subjects who receive treatment for a specified duration, excluding those who discontinue prematurely.

- **Completer Population:** Includes subjects who complete the entire study according to protocol requirements.

3. **Utilization of Population Flags:**

- Population flags ensure consistency in analysis by organizing subjects based on predefined criteria for each population.

- They facilitate subgroup analyses and sensitivity analyses by stratifying subjects into different populations based on specific characteristics or events.

- Population flags support regulatory submissions by documenting the population definitions used for various analyses, enhancing transparency and reproducibility in clinical trial data analysis.

CHAPTER TWENTY-NINE

Baseline Type (BASETYPE)

In clinical research and data analysis, "Baseline Type" (BASETYPE) refers to a variable or parameter that identifies the type or category of baseline data being collected or analyzed within a study or clinical trial. Here's a breakdown:

   1. **Definition**:
- BASETYPE categorizes baseline data according to specific criteria or characteristics relevant to the study design, objectives, or therapeutic area.
- It helps to differentiate between different types of baseline measurements or assessments that may be collected for subjects enrolled in the study.

   if Baseline Value (BASE) is populated, and there is more than one definition of baseline, then BASETYPE must be non-null on all records of any type for that parameter.

   Baseline: Baseline value refers to the last measurement made prior to administration of the first dose of study medication.

   2. **Examples**:
- BASETYPE might include categories such as:
- "Pre-treatment baseline": Baseline measurements taken before the initiation of a treatment or intervention.
- "Post-randomization baseline": Baseline measurements taken after subjects have been randomized into treatment groups but before any treatment is administered.
- "Historical baseline": Baseline data obtained from historical records or databases, rather than from measurements taken specifically for the current study.
- "Screening baseline": Baseline measurements taken during the screening process to assess eligibility criteria for study enrollment.

   3. **Usage**:
- BASETYPE is used to classify and organize baseline data in datasets and analysis outputs, allowing researchers to differentiate between different types of baseline measurements for analysis and interpretation.
- It facilitates subgroup analyses, stratification, or adjustment based on the type of baseline data being considered.

   4. **Implementation**:
- BASETYPE is typically defined and assigned during the data collection or dataset creation phase of a study.
- It may be included as a variable in the dataset, with each observation labeled according to its baseline type.
- Analysis programs or statistical models can then use BASETYPE to appropriately handle and analyze baseline data based on its type.

PARAMCD	ADT	VISIT	AVISIT	ABLFL	ANL01FL	AVAL	BASE	CHG	DTYPE	BASETYPE	PARAMTYP	Row_Categories
ALT	01AUG2012	VISIT 1	SCREENING		Y	2.50	4.10			LAST		Observed
ALT	17AUG2012	VISIT 2	BASELINE			3.04	4.10			LAST		Observed
ALT	17AUG2012	VISIT 2	BASELINE	Y	Y	4.10	4.10			LAST		Observed
ALT	17AUG2012	VISIT 2	AVERAGE BASELINE	Y	Y	3.57	3.57		AVERAGE	AVERAGE		Derived Timepoint
ALT	29AUG2012	VISIT 3	WEEK 2		Y	3.47	4.10	-0.63		LAST		Observed
ALT	14SEP2012	VISIT 4	WEEK 4		Y	4.25	4.10	0.15		LAST		Observed
ALT	26SEP2012	VISIT 6	WEEK 8		Y	5.10	4.10	1.00		LAST		Observed
ALT	29AUG2012	VISIT 3	WEEK 2		Y	3.47	3.57	-0.10		AVERAGE		Alternative Baseline
ALT	14SEP2012	VISIT 4	WEEK 4		Y	4.25	3.57	0.68		AVERAGE		Alternative Baseline
ALT	26SEP2012	VISIT 6	WEEK 8		Y	5.10	3.57	1.53		AVERAGE		Alternative Baseline

What is the CRT (Clinical Study Report) package in clinical trial project submission, and what components does it typically include?

1. **Definition of CRT Package:**
   - The CRT (Clinical Study Report) package is a comprehensive document submitted to regulatory authorities as part of the clinical trial project submission.
   - It provides a detailed summary of the clinical trial, including study design, methodology, results, and conclusions.
   2. **Components of CRT Package:**
   - **Introduction:** Provides background information on the study objectives, rationale, and design.
   - **Study Design:** Describes the study design, including objectives, endpoints, treatment arms, and patient population.
   - **Methods:** Details the study methodology, including patient recruitment, randomization, blinding, and statistical analysis plan.
   - **Results:** Presents the primary and secondary outcomes, safety data, efficacy assessments, and any subgroup analyses.
   - **Discussion:** Interpretation of the study results, comparison with existing literature, and implications for clinical practice.
   - **Conclusion:** Summary of the study findings, including the main conclusions and recommendations.
   - **Appendices:** Supplementary information such as data listings, tables, figures, and additional analyses.
   - **Quality Control and Assurance:** Documentation of quality control measures, including data validation, monitoring, and auditing procedures.
   - **Ethical Considerations:** Documentation of ethical approvals, patient consent forms, and compliance with regulatory requirements.
   - **References:** Citations for relevant literature and previous studies referenced in the report.
   3. **Purpose and Importance:**
   - The CRT package serves as a critical document for regulatory submissions, providing comprehensive information on the conduct and results of the clinical trial.
   - It demonstrates compliance with regulatory requirements and guidelines, ensuring transparency and accountability in the conduct of clinical research.
   - Regulatory authorities use the CRT package to evaluate the safety, efficacy, and quality of the investigational product, informing decisions regarding approval for marketing authorization.

   In summary, the CRT package is a vital component of clinical trial project submission, providing a detailed overview of the study design, methodology, results, and conclusions to regulatory authorities for evaluation and approval.

CHAPTER THIRTY-ONE

Decimal precision and alignment of a laboratory summary statistics table??

Calculated means and medians will be tabulated to one more decimal place than the original data;

Minimum and maximum values will be tabulated to the same number of decimal places as the original data;

Standard deviation will be tabulated to two or more decimal places than the original data;

RULE

USUBJID	LBCAT	LBTESTCD	VISIT	LBDTC	LBORRES
101	HEMATOLOGY	WBC	SCREENING	2018-01-01T09:00:00	9
101	HEMATOLOGY	WBC	DAY1	2018-01-03T09:00:00	9.1
101	HEMATOLOGY	WBC	WEEK1	2018-01-08T09:05:00	3.62
101	HEMATOLOGY	WBC	WEEK2	2018-01-15T09:08:00	4.13
101	HEMATOLOGY	WBC	WEEK4	2018-01-29T09:09:00	4.233
101	HEMATOLOGY	BASO	SCREENING	2018-01-01T09:20:00	1
101	HEMATOLOGY	BASO	DAY1	2018-01-03T09:00:00	2
101	HEMATOLOGY	BASO	WEEK1	2018-01-08T09:10:00	1.22
101	HEMATOLOGY	BASO	WEEK2	2018-01-15T09:07:00	1.1
101	HEMATOLOGY	BASO	WEEK4	2018-01-29T09:05:00	1.02
102	HEMATOLOGY	WBC	SCREENING	2018-01-01T09:00:00	6.02
102	HEMATOLOGY	WBC	DAY1	2018-01-03T09:00:00	2
102	HEMATOLOGY	WBC	WEEK1	2018-01-08T09:05:00	3.6
102	HEMATOLOGY	WBC	WEEK2	2018-01-15T09:08:00	3.9
102	HEMATOLOGY	WBC	WEEK4	2018-01-29T09:09:00	4.2
102	HEMATOLOGY	BASO	SCREENING	2018-01-01T09:20:00	1
102	HEMATOLOGY	BASO	DAY1	2018-01-03T09:00:00	1.11
102	HEMATOLOGY	BASO	WEEK1	2018-01-08T09:10:00	1.2
102	HEMATOLOGY	BASO	WEEK2	2018-01-15T09:07:00	1.11
102	HEMATOLOGY	BASO	WEEK4	2018-01-29T09:05:00	1.01
101	CHEMISTRY	ALT	SCREENING	2018-01-01T09:20:00	13
101	CHEMISTRY	ALT	DAY1	2018-01-03T09:00:00	15
101	CHEMISTRY	ALT	WEEK1	2018-01-08T09:10:00	10
101	CHEMISTRY	ALT	WEEK2	2018-01-15T09:07:00	12
101	CHEMISTRY	ALT	WEEK4	2018-01-29T09:05:00	19

LOOK WBC ALL VALUES DECIMAL HIGHEST IS 3 DECIMALS

LBCAT	LBTESTC	VISIT	n	mean	std	max	median	min	stat	_col2	_col
HEMATOLOGY	BASO	WEEK4	2	1.015	0.007	1.02	1.02	1.01	2	Mean	1.015
HEMATOLOGY	BASO	WEEK4	2	1.015	0.007	1.02	1.02	1.01	3	SD	0.0071
HEMATOLOGY	BASO	WEEK4	2	1.015	0.007	1.02	1.02	1.01	4	Median	1.015
HEMATOLOGY	BASO	WEEK4	2	1.015	0.007	1.02	1.02	1.01	5	Min	1.01
HEMATOLOGY	BASO	WEEK4	2	1.015	0.007	1.02	1.02	1.01	6	Max	1.02
HEMATOLOGY	WBC	DAY1	2	5.55	5.02	9.1	5.55	2	1	N	2
HEMATOLOGY	WBC	DAY1	2	5.55	5.02	9.1	5.55	2	2	Mean	5.5500
HEMATOLOGY	WBC	DAY1	2	5.55	5.02	9.1	5.55	2	3	SD	5.02046
HEMATOLOGY	WBC	DAY1	2	5.55	5.02	9.1	5.55	2	4	Median	5.5500
HEMATOLOGY	WBC	DAY1	2	5.55	5.02	9.1	5.55	2	5	Min	2.000
HEMATOLOGY	WBC	DAY1	2	5.55	5.02	9.1	5.55	2	6	Max	9.100
HEMATOLOGY	WBC	SCREENING	2	7.51	2.107	9	7.51	6.02	1	N	2
HEMATOLOGY	WBC	SCREENING	2	7.51	2.107	9	7.51	6.02	2	Mean	7.5100
HEMATOLOGY	WBC	SCREENING	2	7.51	2.107	9	7.51	6.02	3	SD	2.10718
HEMATOLOGY	WBC	SCREENING	2	7.51	2.107	9	7.51	6.02	4	Median	7.5100
HEMATOLOGY	WBC	SCREENING	2	7.51	2.107	9	7.51	6.02	5	Min	6.020
HEMATOLOGY	WBC	SCREENING	2	7.51	2.107	9	7.51	6.02	6	Max	9.000
HEMATOLOGY	WBC	WEEK1	2	3.61	0.014	3.62	3.61	3.6	1	N	2

CHAPTER THIRTY-TWO

LOCF (Last observation carry forward) WOCF (WORST observation carry forward)

In SAS, LOCF (Last Observation Carry Forward) and WOCF (Worst Observation Carry Forward) are techniques used to handle missing data in longitudinal or time-series datasets. Here's a brief explanation of each:

1. **LOCF (Last Observation Carry Forward)**:

- LOCF imputes missing values by carrying forward the last observed value for each variable.

- This method assumes that the last known value is a reasonable estimate for the missing value until a new observation is recorded.

- LOCF is commonly used in clinical trials or studies where missing data points are expected to remain relatively stable over time.

2. **WOCF (Worst Observation Carry Forward)**:

- WOCF is similar to LOCF but instead of carrying forward the last observation, it carries forward the "worst" observed value.

- The "worst" observation could be defined based on various criteria, such as the highest or lowest observed value.

- WOCF is sometimes used when researchers want to adopt a more conservative approach to imputing missing data, particularly if outliers or extreme values are present in the dataset.

Both LOCF and WOCF are useful techniques for imputing missing data in longitudinal datasets, but they have different implications for data analysis and interpretation. Choosing between them depends on the specific characteristics of the dataset and the research objectives.

Row	USUBJID	VISIT	AVISIT	ADY	PARAM	AVAL	DTYPE	VSSEQ
1	1002	Baseline	Baseline	-4	SUPINE SYSBP (mm Hg)	145		77
2	1002	Week 1	Week 1	3	SUPINE SYSBP (mm Hg)	130		78
3	1002	Week 2	Week 2	9	SUPINE SYSBP (mm Hg)	138		79
4	1002	Week 3	Week 3	18	SUPINE SYSBP (mm Hg)	135		80
5	1002	Week 3	Week 4	18	SUPINE SYSBP (mm Hg)	135	LOCF	80

LOCF

USUBJID	VISIT	AVISIT	ADY	PARAM	AVAL	DTYPE	VSSEQ
1002	Baseline	Baseline	-4	SUPINE SYSBP (mm Hg)	145		77
1002	Week 1	Week 1	3	SUPINE SYSBP (mm Hg)	130		78
1002	Week 2	Week 2	9	SUPINE SYSBP (mm Hg)	138		79
1002	Week 3	Week 3	18	SUPINE SYSBP (mm Hg)	135		80
1002	Week 3	Week 4	18	SUPINE SYSBP (mm Hg)	135	LOCF	80
1002	Week 2	Week 4	9	SUPINE SYSBP (mm Hg)	138	WOCF	79
1002	Week 5	Week 5	33	SUPINE SYSBP (mm Hg)	130		81

WOCF

What are the differences between Phase I, Phase II, and Phase III clinical trials?

Phase I Clinical Trials: Phase I trials are the initial stage of clinical trials in drug development. They primarily focus on evaluating the safety and tolerability of a new drug or treatment in a small group of healthy volunteers or patients with the target condition. Phase I trials also aim to determine the optimal dosage and dosing schedule for the drug. These trials typically involve a small number of participants (usually fewer than 100) and are relatively short in duration. The primary outcome measures in Phase I trials are safety and pharmacokinetics.

- **Phase II Clinical Trials**: Phase II trials follow Phase I trials and are designed to further evaluate the safety and preliminary efficacy of the drug or treatment. They involve a larger group of participants (typically several hundred) who have the target condition. Phase II trials aim to gather more information about the drug's effectiveness and potential side effects, as well as to refine dosage and dosing regimens. The primary outcome measures in Phase II trials are still safety and efficacy, but they are more focused than in Phase I trials.

- **Phase III Clinical Trials**: Phase III trials are large-scale studies conducted after Phase II trials to confirm the findings from earlier phases and to assess the overall benefit-risk profile of the drug. They involve a much larger number of participants (often thousands) and are conducted across multiple sites and geographic regions. Phase III trials compare the new drug or treatment to standard treatments or placebo and aim to provide the data necessary for regulatory approval. The primary outcome measures in Phase III trials are efficacy and long-term safety.

In summary, Phase I trials focus on safety and dosage determination in a small group of participants, Phase II trials further evaluate safety and preliminary efficacy in a larger group, and Phase III trials confirm efficacy and safety in a large population to support regulatory approval.

Clinical Trials

Enter Caption

CHAPTER THIRTY-FOUR

What is Pinnacle 21, and how is it utilized in clinical SAS projects?

Overview of Pinnacle 21:

Pinnacle 21 is a **software platform** designed for data quality management and validation in clinical research.

It offers a suite of tools and modules specifically tailored for assessing and improving the quality of clinical trial data.

Utilization in Clinical SAS Projects:

Pinnacle 21 is commonly utilized in clinical SAS projects to perform comprehensive data validation checks and ensure compliance with regulatory standards.

It provides automated checks for common data quality issues, such as missing values, inconsistent data formats, and out-of-range values.

Pinnacle 21 allows SAS programmers and data managers to create customized validation rules and checks based on specific project requirements and regulatory guidelines.

The platform generates detailed reports highlighting data discrepancies, errors, and warnings identified during the validation process, enabling users to prioritize and address issues efficiently.

Pinnacle 21 facilitates collaboration among team members by providing centralized access to validation results and allowing for tracking of validation activities and resolutions.

Ultimately, Pinnacle 21 helps streamline the data validation process, improves data quality, and ensures the integrity and reliability of clinical trial data for regulatory submissions.

Pinnacle 21 Validator Report

Configuration: G:\My Journey Drive\MyYouTubeLibrary\12_MY YOUTUBE\5 classes upcoming\Vaishali\components\config\SDTM 3.2.xml
Define.xml: G:\My Journey Drive\MyYouTubeLibrary\12_MY YOUTUBE\5 classes upcoming\Vaishali
Generated: 2024-03-13T18:10:47
CDISC CT Version: 2016-06-24
UNII Version: 2016-09-06
NDF-RT Version: 2016-09-08
Software Version: 2.2.0

Issue Summary

Source	Pinnacle 21 ID	Publisher ID	Message	Severity	Found
AE					
	SD1082	FDAC036	Variable length is too long for actual data	Error	18
	SD1076	FDAC031	Model permissible variable added into standard domain	Warning	1
	SD1097	FDAC022	No Treatment Emergent info for Adverse Event	Warning	2
CM					
	SD1082	FDAC036	Variable length is too long for actual data	Error	14
	CT2002	FDAC341	CMDOSU value not found in 'Unit' extensible codelist	Warning	1
	SD1076	FDAC031	Model permissible variable added into standard domain	Warning	1
CO					
	SD1082	FDAC036	Variable length is too long for actual data	Error	4
	SD1021	FDAC216	Unexpected character value in COVAL variable	Warning	34
	SD1076	FDAC031	Model permissible variable added into standard domain	Warning	1
	SD0063A	FDAC033	SDTM/dataset variable label mismatch	Notice	1
DM					
	CT2001	FDAC340	DTHFL value not found in 'No Yes Response (Yes only)' non-extensible codelist	Error	48
	SD1001	FDAC048	Duplicate SUBJID	Error	2
	SD1082	FDAC036	Variable length is too long for actual data	Error	18
	SD0002	FDAC113	No baseline result in EG for subject	Warning	1

How can the %SYSFUNC function be utilized in SAS code, and what are some examples of its application?

1. **Functionality of %SYSFUNC:**

- The %SYSFUNC function in SAS enables the execution of external functions or routines within SAS code, allowing integration of non-SAS functions into SAS programs.

- It provides a way to call functions from other programming languages, such as SQL, Excel, or even user-defined functions, and incorporate their results into SAS code.

2. **Examples of %SYSFUNC Usage:**

- **Example 1: Calling a System Function:**

```
data _null_;
length os_version $100;
os_version = %sysfunc(getoption(SYSSCP));
put "Operating System Version: " os_version;
run;
```

Explanation: In this example, the %SYSFUNC function is used to call the GETOPTION function, which retrieves the value of the SYSSCP option (operating system information). The retrieved information is then assigned to the variable OS_VERSION and printed to the SAS log.

- **Example 2: Using External Functions:**

```
data example;
set mydata;
new_variable = %sysfunc(max(var1, var2));
run;
```

Explanation: Here, the %SYSFUNC function is utilized to call the MAX function, a non-SAS function, to find the maximum value between VAR1 and VAR2 within a SAS data step. The result is assigned to the variable NEW_VARIABLE.

3. **Benefits of %SYSFUNC:**

- **Flexibility:** %SYSFUNC enhances the flexibility of SAS programming by allowing integration of external functions or routines, expanding the capabilities of SAS code.

- **Efficiency:** It enables the use of specialized functions or routines from other programming languages without the need for extensive data manipulation or preprocessing.

- **Customization:** %SYSFUNC facilitates customization and advanced data processing tasks by incorporating user-defined functions or system functions into SAS programs.

In summary, the %SYSFUNC function in SAS provides a powerful mechanism for calling external functions or routines within SAS code, offering increased flexibility, efficiency, and customization options for data processing and analysis.

What are local and global macro variables in SAS, and how do they differ in their scope and usage?

1. **Local Macro Variables:**

- Local macro variables are defined within a specific SAS program or macro and are only accessible within that scope.

- They are typically created using the %LET statement and are prefixed with an ampersand (&) when referenced.

- Local macro variables cease to exist once the SAS program or macro where they are defined finishes executing.

- They are useful for storing temporary values or parameters within a specific portion of code without affecting other parts of the program.

2. **Global Macro Variables:**

- Global macro variables are defined outside of any specific SAS program or macro and are accessible throughout the entire SAS session.

- They are typically created using the %LET statement with the GLOBAL option, or by defining them in an autocall macro or autocall library.

- Global macro variables persist across different SAS programs, macros, and sessions until they are explicitly deleted or overwritten.

- They are useful for storing values or parameters that need to be shared and accessed across multiple SAS programs or macros within a session.

Example:

```
/* Local Macro Variable Example */
%macro local_example;
%local x;
%let x = 10;
%put Local Macro Variable x: &x;
%mend local_example;
/* Global Macro Variable Example */
%let global_var = 20;
%macro global_example;
%put Global Macro Variable global_var: &global_var;
%mend global_example;
/* Calling Macros */
%local_example;
%global_example;
```

Output:

```
Local Macro Variable x: 10
```

Global Macro Variable global_var: 20

In this example, the local macro variable `x` is defined within the `local_example` macro and is only accessible within that macro. In contrast, the global macro variable `global_var` is defined outside of any specific macro and can be accessed from anywhere within the SAS session.

CHAPTER THIRTY-SEVEN

What is the purpose of FMTSEARCH in SAS?

```
/* FMTSEARCH in SAS */
    /* The FMTSEARCH system option specifies the search path for SAS formats. */
    /* Example: */
    options fmtsearch=(work.formats lib.formats);
```

The purpose of the FMTSEARCH option is to specify the search path that SAS uses to locate user-defined formats. When SAS encounters a variable with a format, it looks for that format in the specified locations. If the format is found, SAS applies it to the variable; if not, SAS issues a warning or an error, depending on the situation.

In the provided example, the FMTSEARCH option is set to `(work.formats lib.formats)`, which means SAS first searches for the format in the WORK library, specifically in the FORMATS catalog within it. If the format is not found there, SAS then searches in the LIB library, again specifically within the FORMATS catalog.

By setting the FMTSEARCH option, users can ensure that SAS can find and apply the appropriate formats to the data, thus enhancing data analysis and reporting capabilities.

What is the function of SASAUTOS in SAS?

/* SASAUTOS in SAS */
  /* The SASAUTOS system option specifies directories where SAS searches for autocall macro programs. */
  /* Example: */
  options sasautos=("c:\sas\macros" "d:\user\macros");

The function of SASAUTOS is to specify directories where SAS searches for autocall macro programs. Autocall macros are stored in external files and automatically compiled and executed when referenced in SAS code.

In the example provided, the SASAUTOS option is set to `("c:\sas\macros" "d:\user\macros")`, indicating that SAS will search for autocall macro programs in the directories `c:\sas\macros` and `d:\user\macros`.

By setting SASAUTOS, users can organize their autocall macros into specific directories and make them readily available for use in SAS programs, thereby enhancing code modularity and efficiency.

CHAPTER THIRTY-NINE

What is the difference between MLOGIC and MPRINT in SAS?

/* MPRINT */
/* MPRINT **displays macro statements** generated by macro execution in the SAS log. */
options mprint;
/* MLOGIC */
/* MLOGIC **displays messages** about the execution of macro statements in the SAS log. */
options mlogic;

The main difference between MLOGIC and MPRINT in SAS lies in the type of information they display in the SAS log:

- **MPRINT:** This option displays the actual macro statements generated by macro execution. It shows the SAS code that is produced after macro variables have been resolved and macro logic has been applied. MPRINT is useful for understanding how macro code is expanded and executed.

- **MLOGIC:** Unlike MPRINT, MLOGIC provides messages about the execution of macro statements. It displays information about the steps involved in processing macro code, such as the beginning and end of macro execution and any error messages encountered during macro compilation. MLOGIC helps in tracking the flow of control within macros and identifying any issues or errors in macro logic.

CHAPTER FORTY

How to find the last date of a month. YYYY-MM-_ _ ??

To find the last date of a month in SAS using the **INTNX** function, you can specify a positive interval of "month" and use the "E" alignment option to get the end of the interval. Here's how you can do it:

/ Define the date you want to find the last date of the month for */*
data _null_;
/ Input date in YYYY-MM format */*
input date yymmn6.;
/ Use INTNX function to find last date of the month */*
last_day_of_month = intnx('month', date, 1, 'E');
/ Format the result */*
format last_day_of_month yymmdd10.;
/ Output result */*
put last_day_of_month= yymmdd10.;
datalines;
2024-05
;
run;

In this example:

*The **INTNX** function is used to add a positive interval of "month" to the input date.*

The "E" option aligns the result to the end of the interval, giving you the last date of the month.

The FORMAT statement is used to format the result in the desired YYYY-MM-DD format.

You can change the date variable to the specific date you want to find the last day of the month for. This example assumes the input date is in the format YYYY-MM. Adjust the format in the INPUT statement accordingly if your input date format is different.

CHAPTER FORTY-ONE

How can you convert rows to columns and vice versa in SAS?

```
/* Converting Rows to Columns */
   /* Using PROC TRANSPOSE */
   proc transpose data=your_dataset out=transposed_rows_to_columns(rename=(col1=new_column_name));
   by id_variable; /* Optional: if you have an identifier variable */
   var variable_of_interest; /* Specify the variable you want to transpose */
   run;
   /* Converting Columns to Rows */
   /* Using PROC TRANSPOSE */
   proc transpose data=your_dataset out=transposed_columns_to_rows(rename=(col1=new_column_name));
   by id_variable; /* Optional: if you have an identifier variable */
   var variable_of_interest; /* Specify the variables you want to transpose */
   run;
```

In SAS, you can convert rows to columns and vice versa using the `PROC TRANSPOSE` procedure. When converting rows to columns, each row of data becomes a column in the transposed dataset. Conversely, when converting columns to rows, each column of data becomes a row in the transposed dataset.

In both cases, you specify the input dataset (`your_dataset`) and use the `VAR` statement to indicate the variable(s) you want to transpose. Optionally, you can use the `BY` statement if you have an identifier variable. The `OUT` statement specifies the name of the transposed dataset.

This approach provides a straightforward method for restructuring data to meet your analytical needs, allowing you to manipulate and analyze data more effectively in SAS.

To add page numbers to a table in SAS, you typically use a combination of SAS output procedures and additional features like the `ODS` (Output Delivery System). Here's a general approach:

```
/* Define the output destination and options */
ods pdf file="output.pdf" startpage=never; /* Output to PDF */
/* Your SAS procedure to generate the table */
proc print data=your_dataset; /* For example */
run;
/* Add page numbers using FOOTNOTE statement */
ods pdf text="&syspagnum" /* Page number */
style=footer font_size=8pt; /* Customize font size, style, etc. */
/* Close the output destination */
ods pdf close;
```

In this code:

- `ODS PDF` sets up the output destination as a PDF file named "output.pdf". The `startpage=never` option ensures that page numbering starts from the first page of the document.

- The SAS procedure (`PROC PRINT` in this example) generates the table.

- The `ODS PDF TEXT` statement adds the page numbers to the bottom of each page using the `&syspagnum` macro variable, which automatically inserts the current page number.

- Customize the appearance of the page numbers by adjusting options like `style`, `font_size`, etc.

- Finally, `ODS PDF CLOSE` closes the output destination.

This code will produce a PDF file with the table and page numbers included at the bottom of each page. You can adapt this approach to other output formats supported by SAS, such as HTML or RTF, by changing the `ODS` destination and options accordingly.

CHAPTER FORTY-TWO

What is the difference between `order=internal` and `order=formatted` in SAS?

In SAS, `order=internal` and `order=formatted` are options used with the `proc sort` procedure to specify the order in which the data is sorted.

- `order=internal` sorts the data based on the internal representation of the values. This means that SAS sorts the data based on how it is stored in the computer's memory, which may not necessarily be in a human-readable format. This option is generally faster than `order=formatted` because it doesn't involve any formatting.

- `order=formatted` sorts the data based on its formatted representation. This means that SAS sorts the data based on how it appears when displayed, considering any associated formats. It may involve additional processing time compared to `order=internal` because it needs to apply formatting rules before sorting.

Example SAS code:

```
/* Sample dataset */
data have;
input ID $ Value;
datalines;
A 10
B 5
C 20
D 15
;
/* Sorting data using order=internal */
proc sort data=have out=sorted_internal order=internal;
by Value;
run;
/* Sorting data using order=formatted */
proc sort data=have out=sorted_formatted order=formatted;
by Value;
run;
```

In this example, `sorted_internal` and `sorted_formatted` will contain the same data but sorted differently based on the `order=` option used.

Sure, here's the modified response displayed like above:

CHAPTER FORTY-THREE

What option will you use when there are missing records?

When dealing with missing records in SAS, you can handle them using the `MISSING` option within the `PROC SORT` procedure. This option allows you to specify how missing values should be treated during sorting.

Here's how you can use it:

```
/* Sample dataset with missing values */
data have;
input ID $ Value;
datalines;
A 10
B .
C 20
D 15
E .
;
/* Sorting data and handling missing values */
proc sort data=have out=sorted_missing missing=last;
by Value;
run;
```

In this example, the `missing=last` option is used to specify that missing values should be treated as larger than any non-missing values during sorting. Alternatively, you can use `missing=first` to treat missing values as smaller than any non-missing values.

CHAPTER FORTY-FOUR

What is the difference between `RETAIN` and `LAG` in SAS?

In SAS, both `RETAIN` and `LAG` are used to retain values across iterations or observations, but they serve different purposes.

- `RETAIN` is a statement used within a data step to retain the value of a variable across iterations of the data step. It initializes the variable's value at the beginning of the data step, and that value persists until explicitly changed or until the end of the data step.

- `LAG` is a function used to access the value of a variable from a previous observation. It returns the value of a variable from the previous observation in the data set. Unlike `RETAIN`, which retains the value within the same iteration, `LAG` accesses the value from a previous observation.

Example SAS code:

```
/* Example using RETAIN */
data example_retain;
retain sum 0;
set input_data;
sum + value;
run;
/* Example using LAG */
data example_lag;
set input_data;
lag_value = lag(value);
run;
```

In the first example, `RETAIN` is used to accumulate a sum across observations. In the second example, `LAG` is used to create a new variable containing the value of `value` from the previous observation.

CHAPTER FORTY-FIVE

What is meant by PDV?

In SAS, PDV stands for Program Data Vector. It's an internal data structure used during the compilation and execution of a DATA step. The PDV is essentially a buffer that holds one observation of a SAS dataset at a time during the execution of a DATA step. It includes the variables defined in the DATA step along with their current values.

When you define variables in a DATA step, SAS allocates space in the PDV for each variable. As the DATA step reads input data or assigns values to variables, it updates the values in the PDV accordingly. At the end of the DATA step, the PDV is written to the output dataset.

Understanding the PDV is crucial for understanding how data manipulation and transformations work in SAS. It's especially important for tasks like creating new variables, updating existing variables, and filtering observations.

Here's a simple example to illustrate the concept:

data example;
input ID $ Value;
if Value > 10 then Category = 'High';
else Category = 'Low';
datalines;
A 5
B 15
C 8
;
run;

In this example, during the execution of the DATA step, the PDV holds the values of `ID`, `Value`, and `Category` for each observation. The `if` statement updates the value of `Category` based on the value of `Value` for each observation. Once the DATA step completes, the PDV is written to the output dataset `example`.

CHAPTER FORTY-SIX

Proc Report with 0 observation dataset

If you want to use a macro variable to count the number of observations in a dataset, including datasets with zero observations, you can use a combination of PROC SQL and the INTO clause to assign the count to a macro variable

```
PROC SQL NOPRINT;
SELECT  COUNT(*) INTO:N_Obs FROM SASHELP.CLASS
WHERE SEX=UPCASE("U");
QUIT;
%PUT &N Obs;
```

```
51    %PUT &N_Obs;
0
```

```sas
%MACRO REP();
ODS LISTING CLOSE;
ODS RTF file="E:\YTREP/un.rtf"
style=sasweb ;
%IF &N_Obs=0 &THEN
%DO;
DATA NoObs;
txt="No Observations in this report";
RUN;
PROC REPORT DATA=NoObs;
COLUMN txt;
DEFINE txt / ' ';
TITLE1 "Gender of the subjects";
RUN;
%END;
```

CHAPTER FORTY-SEVEN

Have you used Proc Append?

Yes, I'm familiar with the `PROC APPEND` procedure in SAS. It's used to append one or more SAS datasets to the end of another SAS dataset. This procedure is particularly useful when you want to combine datasets vertically (i.e., add observations) without having to re-create the structure of the target dataset.

Here's a basic example of how `PROC APPEND` is used:

```
/* Create two sample datasets */
data dataset1;
input ID $ Value;
datalines;
A 10
B 15
;
run;
data dataset2;
input ID $ Value;
datalines;
C 20
D 25
;
run;
/* Append dataset2 to dataset1 */
proc append base=dataset1 data=dataset2 force;
run;
```

In this example, `dataset2` is appended to the end of `dataset1`. The `FORCE` option is used to overwrite `dataset1` if it already exists and to create it if it does not exist.

CHAPTER FORTY-EIGHT

What is the difference between length in merge in SAS?

In SAS, the term "length" can refer to two different concepts: the LENGTH statement and the LENGTH function.

- The LENGTH statement is used to explicitly define the length of variables in a dataset, specifying the maximum length of character variables or the number of bytes for numeric variables. This statement is typically used in data step programming to pre-allocate memory space for variables.

- On the other hand, the LENGTH function is used to determine the length of a character variable's value at execution time. It returns the length of the character string in bytes, which can be useful for dynamic manipulation of character variables.

While neither the LENGTH statement nor the LENGTH function directly affects the merge operation in SAS, it's important to ensure that the variables being merged have compatible lengths to avoid truncation or data loss during the merge process. If necessary, you can use the LENGTH statement to explicitly define the lengths of variables before merging datasets.

CHAPTER FORTY-NINE

What is PROC IMPORT in SAS, and how is it used to import external data into a SAS dataset?

PROC IMPORT is a SAS procedure designed to import external data files, such as CSV, Excel, or delimited text files, into SAS datasets. It automatically detects the format of the external file and generates SAS code to read and import the data. Users specify the datafile location, the desired SAS dataset name, and additional options such as the DBMS (Data Base Management System) type and whether to replace existing datasets. This procedure streamlines the process of importing external data, making it easier for SAS users to work with diverse data sources within their SAS environment.

```
/* Import CSV file using PROC IMPORT */
proc import datafile='C:\Data\data.csv'
out=mydataset
dbms=csv
replace;
run;
```

In this example:

- `datafile='C:\Data\data.csv'` specifies the path to the CSV file to be imported.
- `out=mydataset` specifies the name of the SAS dataset to be created.
- `dbms=csv` indicates that the external file is in CSV format.
- `replace` replaces any existing dataset with the same name.

How can data quality and integrity be ensured in SAS?

Data quality and integrity in SAS can be ensured through various techniques and procedures:

1. **PROC CONTENTS**: This procedure provides information about dataset characteristics such as the number of observations, variables, and variable attributes like length and type.

2. **PROC FREQ**: Use PROC FREQ to generate frequency tables, which reveal counts of unique values for each variable, aiding in the detection of unexpected or missing data points.

3. **PROC MEANS**: Employ PROC MEANS to compute summary statistics like mean, median, and minimum/maximum values, facilitating the identification of outliers or unusual data.

4. **PROC SQL**: Utilize PROC SQL to perform comprehensive data validation checks using SQL queries. These checks can include identifying duplicate records, missing values, or inconsistencies between variables.

5. **Data Step**: Write custom data step code to execute specific data validation tasks, such as identifying outliers or ensuring the validity of relationships between variables.

By employing these methods, data analysts can ensure that the data used for analysis is of high quality, consistent, and reliable, thus enhancing the credibility of analytical insights and decision-making processes.

CHAPTER FIFTY-ONE

What is the difference between the chi-square test and Fisher's exact test for calculating p-values?

Both the chi-square test and Fisher's exact test are used to assess the association between categorical variables, but they differ in their methodologies and applicability.

- **Chi-Square Test**: The chi-square test is based on the chi-square distribution and is commonly used to determine if there is a significant association between two categorical variables. It calculates the expected frequencies under the assumption of independence between the variables and compares them to the observed frequencies. The test is suitable for larger sample sizes and approximates the null distribution of the test statistic.

- **Fisher's Exact Test**: Fisher's exact test calculates the exact probability of observing the data under the null hypothesis of independence. It is particularly useful when dealing with small sample sizes or when the assumptions of the chi-square test are violated. Fisher's exact test provides an exact p-value, making it more reliable in such scenarios.

Here's how you can perform both tests in SAS:

```
/* Chi-Square Test */
proc freq data=mydata;
tables variable1*variable2 / chisq;
run;
/* Fisher's Exact Test */
proc freq data=mydata;
tables variable1*variable2 / exact;
run;
```

In both examples, replace `mydata`, `variable1`, and `variable2` with the appropriate dataset name and variable names from your data. The `CHISQ` option in the first `PROC FREQ` call specifies that you want to perform a chi-square test, while the `EXACT` option in the second `PROC FREQ` call specifies Fisher's exact test.

Describe the validation procedure? How would you perform the validation for TLG as well as analysis data set?

Validation procedure is used to check the output of the SAS program, generated by the source programmer. In this process validator write the program and generate the output. If this output is same as the output generated by the SAS programmer's output then the program is considered to be valid. We can perform this validation for TLG by checking the output manually and for analysis data set it can be done using PROC COMPARE.

Certainly! Here's how you might express the validation process using SAS syntax:

/ Validation Program */*
/ Step 1: Define the reference dataset */*
data reference;
/ Code to create reference dataset */*
run;
/ Step 2: Generate output using validation program */*
proc <PROCEDURE> data=<DATASET_USED_BY_PROGRAM>;
/ Code to generate output */*
run;
/ Step 3: Compare output with reference dataset */*
proc compare base=reference compare=<OUTPUT_FROM_STEP_2>;
/ Options for comparison, such as variables to include/exclude */*
run;

In this syntax:

- Replace `<PROCEDURE>` with the appropriate SAS procedure used to generate output in the validation program (e.g., PROC MEANS, PROC FREQ, etc.).
- Replace `<DATASET_USED_BY_PROGRAM>` with the dataset used by the source programmer's SAS program.
- Replace `<OUTPUT_FROM_STEP_2>` with the output dataset generated by the validation program.
- Modify and add additional options within the PROC COMPARE step as needed to customize the comparison (e.g., specifying variables to include/exclude, tolerance levels for numeric comparisons, etc.).

This structure outlines the typical steps involved in a SAS validation process, where output generated by the validation program is compared against a reference dataset to ensure accuracy.

How would you perform the validation for the listing, which has 400 pages?

It is not possible to perform the validation for the listing having 400 pages manually. To do this, we convert the listing in data sets by using PROC RTF and then after that we can compare it by using PROC COMPARE.

Visit windowing ANL01FL ?????

It seems like you've mentioned several terms: "VISIT," "WINDOWING," and "ANL01FL." Let's break down each term:

    1. **VISIT**:

- In clinical trials and research studies, a "visit" refers to a scheduled encounter between a subject or participant and the study staff.
- Each visit typically involves specific activities, such as data collection, assessments, treatments, or follow-ups.
- Visits are organized according to a predefined schedule, often outlined in the study protocol, and can vary in frequency and duration depending on the study design and objectives.

    2. **WINDOWING**:

- "Windowing" in the context of clinical research usually refers to the concept of allowing flexibility around the timing of study visits or assessments.
- It involves defining acceptable ranges or windows within which visits or assessments can occur without being considered late or missed.
- Windowing helps accommodate practical challenges, such as scheduling conflicts or logistical issues, while still maintaining data integrity and study adherence.
- For example, a study might specify that a visit scheduled for Day 30 can occur within a window of ±2 days, meaning it can take place between Day 28 and Day 32 without being considered overdue.

    3. **ANL01FL**:

- "ANL01FL" appears to be a code or identifier that may refer to a specific variable, dataset, or analysis file within the context of a clinical study or research project.
- Without further context, it's challenging to provide a specific interpretation of "ANL01FL." It could represent a particular data file, analysis result, or variable name used in statistical analysis.

    If you could provide more details or context about "ANL01FL" or clarify your question, I'd be happy to provide further assistance!

Row	PARAM	AVISIT	AVISITN	VISITNUM	VSSEQ	ABLFL	AVAL	BASE	CHG	DTYPE	ADY	AWTARGET	AWTDIFF	ANL01FL
1	Systolic BP (mm Hg)	Screening	-4	1	3821		120	114	.		-30	-28	2	Y
2	Systolic BP (mm Hg)	Run-In	-2	2	3822		116	114	.		-16	-14	2	Y
3	Systolic BP (mm Hg)	Week 0	0	3	3823	Y	114	114	0		-2	1	2	Y
4	Systolic BP (mm Hg)	Week 2	2	4	3824		118	114	4		13	14	1	Y
5	Systolic BP (mm Hg)	Week 2	2	4.1	3825		126	114	12		17	14	3	
6	Systolic BP (mm Hg)	Week 4	4	5	3826		122	114	8		23	28	5	Y
7	Systolic BP (mm Hg)	Week 8	8	5	3826		122	114	8	LOCF	23	56	33	Y
8	Systolic BP (mm Hg)	Week 8	8	4.1	3825		126	114	12	WOCF	17	56	39	Y
9	Systolic BP (mm Hg)	Week 12	12	7	3827		134	114	20		83	84	1	Y

AWTARGET = Planned Study Day from SDTM,
AWTARGET   Analysis Window Target
AWTDIFF is the absolute value of ADY - AWTARGET,
AWTDIFF   Analysis Window Diff from Target
ANL01FL is used in this study to identify the record selected for analysis when there are
multiple records for a given AVISIT

How do you Rename all variables in a dataset when you have large number of variables.??

When you have a large number of variables in a dataset and you want to rename all of them, it's more efficient to use an automated method rather than renaming each variable manually. In SAS, you can use a combination of PROC DATASETS and a macro to rename variables programmatically. Here's how you can do it:

```
/* Example Dataset */
data original_dataset;
/* Your data step code to create the original dataset */
run;
    /* Create a macro to rename variables */
%macro rename_vars(lib=, ds=, prefix=);
/* Get the list of variables in the dataset */
proc contents data=&lib..&ds out=vars noprint;
run;
    /* Use a data step to rename variables */
data &lib..&ds (rename=(
%do i = 1 %to &sqlobs;
%let var = %scan(vars, &i);
%trim(&var)=&prefix.&var
%if &i < &sqlobs %then %str(,)
%end;
));
set &lib..&ds;
run;
    /* Delete the temporary dataset containing variable information */
proc datasets library=&lib nolist;
delete vars;
run;
%mend rename_vars;
    /* Call the macro to rename variables */
%rename_vars(lib=work, ds=original_dataset, prefix=new_);
    /* Check the renamed dataset */
proc contents data=work.original_dataset;
run;
```

Replace **original_dataset** with the name of your dataset.

Specify the **lib** parameter with the library where your dataset resides.

Specify the **prefix** parameter with the prefix you want to add to each variable name.

This macro renames all variables in the dataset by adding the specified prefix to their names.

The **proc contents** step retrieves the list of variables in the dataset.

The macro **%rename_vars** then renames each variable by appending the specified prefix.

Finally, the temporary dataset containing variable information is deleted.

This approach allows you to rename all variables in a dataset programmatically, saving time and effort when dealing with large datasets.

CHAPTER FIFTY-SIX

Criterion Flags in ADaM ????

In the ADaM (Analysis Data Model) methodology, the use of an analysis criterion variable, CRITy, along with a criterion evaluation result flag, CRITyFL, is essential for identifying whether a specific criterion is met. Here's an explanation of each:

   1. **CRITy (Criterion Variable):**
- CRITy represents the analysis criterion or condition that needs to be evaluated.
- It could be a threshold, rule, or condition against which data is compared or evaluated.
- For example, CRITy could be a cutoff value for a laboratory parameter, a specific event occurrence, or a predefined criteria for treatment response.
- CRITy is typically defined based on the requirements of the analysis or study objectives.

   2. **CRITyFL (Criterion Evaluation Result Flag):**
- CRITyFL is a flag variable used to indicate the evaluation result of the criterion specified by CRITy.
- It is a binary flag that indicates whether the criterion is met or not for each observation in the dataset.
- Common values for CRITyFL might include 1 for "Criterion Met" and 0 for "Criterion Not Met."
- CRITyFL allows for easy identification and filtering of observations based on whether they satisfy the specified criterion.

Together, CRITy and CRITyFL provide a standardized approach for evaluating and documenting the fulfillment of analysis criteria within ADaM datasets. They facilitate transparency, reproducibility, and consistency in data analysis processes, ensuring that criteria are applied uniformly across different analyses and studies.

Row	USUBJID	PARAM	AVAL	BASE	CHG	CRIT1	CRIT1FL
1	1001	Systolic Blood Pressure (mm Hg)	163	148	15	Systolic Pressure >160 and Change from Baseline in Systolic Pressure>10	Y
2	1002	Systolic Blood Pressure (mm Hg)	140	148	-8	Systolic Pressure >160 and Change from Baseline in Systolic Pressure>10	N
3	1005	Systolic Blood Pressure (mm Hg)	120			Systolic Pressure >160 and Change from Baseline in Systolic Pressure>10	

CHAPTER FIFTY-SEVEN

SPARSE (VS) PRELOADFMT ??

In SAS, "SPARSE" and "PRELOADFMT" are attributes associated with formats in the FORMAT procedure (`PROC FORMAT`). Here's what each term means:

1. **SPARSE**:
- In the context of SAS formats, "SPARSE" is an option that controls how the format is stored in memory.
- When SPARSE is specified, SAS stores the format in a more memory-efficient manner, particularly when the format has many defined values but only a subset of those values are actually used in the dataset.
- Sparse formats save memory by not allocating space for unused format values, which can be advantageous when dealing with large datasets or formats with many possible values but few actual occurrences.

2. **PRELOADFMT**:
- "PRELOADFMT" is an option in the FORMAT procedure (`PROC FORMAT`) that specifies whether SAS should preload a format into memory when the procedure is invoked.
- When PRELOADFMT is specified, SAS loads the format into memory at the beginning of the session or when the procedure is executed, making the format immediately available for use.
- Preloading formats can improve performance by reducing the time needed to access format information during data processing.

In summary, SPARSE controls how SAS stores formats in memory, optimizing memory usage by not allocating space for unused format values. PRELOADFMT determines whether SAS should preload formats into memory, potentially improving performance by making format information readily accessible during data processing. Both attributes are important considerations when working with SAS formats, particularly in scenarios involving large datasets or frequent format usage.

```
PROC FORMAT;
  VALUE $trt
  "PLB"="Placebo"
  "AT1"="Active drug 1"
  "AT2"="Active drug 2"
  ;
  VALUE $sex
  "M"="Male"
  "F"="Female"
  "U"="Undifferentiated"
  ;
  RUN;

  /* Execute PROC FREQ with sparse option to get the counts*/
PROC FREQ DATA=demog;
  TABLES treatment*sex/sparse out=count2 (drop=percent);
  FORMAT treatment $trt. Sex $sex.;
  RUN;
```

	treatment	sex	COUNT
1	Active drug 1	Female	2
2	Active drug 1	Male	0
3	Placebo	Female	1
4	Placebo	Male	3

```
PROC FORMAT;
VALUE $trt
"PLB"="Placebo"
"AT1"="Active drug 1"
"AT2"="Active drug 2"
;
VALUE $sex
"M"="Male"
"F"="Female"
"U"="Undifferentiated"
;
RUN;

/* Execute PROC TABULATE AND PRELOADFMT  option to get the counts*/


options missing=0 ;

PROC TABULATE DATA=demog  out=count2 (drop=_TYPE_ _PAGE_ _TABLE_);
 class treatment sex/preloadfmt;
 format sex $sex. treatment $trt.;
 table  treatment*sex /printmiss  ;
RUN;
```

	treatment	sex	N
1	Active drug 1	Female	2
2	Active drug 1	Male	0
3	Active drug 1	Undifferentiated	0
4	Active drug 2	Female	0
5	Active drug 2	Male	0
6	Active drug 2	Undifferentiated	0
7	Placebo	Female	1
8	Placebo	Male	3
9	Placebo	Undifferentiated	0

CHAPTER FIFTY-EIGHT

How to Merge the SUPP Domain to Main Domain in ADaM??

1. **Sort Datasets**:
- First, sort both the main domain dataset (`main_domain`) and the supplementary domain dataset (`supp_domain`) by a common identifier variable (e.g., subject identifier).
   2. **Merge Datasets**:
- Use the `MERGE` statement to combine the observations from both datasets based on the common identifier variable.
- Specify the `BY` statement to indicate the variable used for merging.
- Ensure that you only include observations from the main domain dataset (`main_domain`) using a conditional statement (e.g., `IF a;`).
   3. **Select Variables**:
- Keep only the variables you need from both domains in the merged dataset (`merged_data`).
- You can use the `RENAME=` option in the `MERGE` statement to rename variables from the supplementary domain if there are naming conflicts with variables from the main domain.
   Here's the SAS code implementing the above steps:

```
/* Step 1: Sort datasets */
proc sort data=main_domain;
by subject_identifier;
run;
   proc sort data=supp_domain;
by subject_identifier;
run;
   /* Step 2: Merge datasets */
data merged_data;
merge main_domain (in=a) supp_domain (in=b);
by subject_identifier;
if a;
run;
```

   Adjust the code according to your dataset names, variable names, and specific requirements for merging the SUPP domain with the main domain in ADaM.

```
proc sort data=suppae1;
   by usubjid aeseq;
run;


proc transpose data=suppae1
out=suppae1_t (drop=_name_ _label_);
   by usubjid aeseq;
   id qnam;
   var qval;
run;
```

	USUBJID	aeseq	AECON
1	765/15-001-S44	1	Y
2	765/15-001-S46	1	Y

```
data ae1;
   merge sdtm.ae (in=a)
         suppae1_t;
   by usubjid aeseq;
   run;
```

STUDYID	DOMAIN	USUBJID	AESEQ	AECON	AEBODSYS	AEDECOD	AETERM
765/15	AE	765/15-001-S44		1 Y	General disorders and administration site conditions	Oedema	OEDEMASIN LEFTUPPERLIMB
765/15	AE	765/15-001-S46		1 Y	Skin and subcutaneous tissue disorders	Rash	RASHES

Area under the curve (AUC) ???

1. **Definition**:
- The AUC is a pharmacokinetic parameter that quantifies the total exposure of the body to a drug over time.
- It represents the integral of the drug concentration in the plasma over time after administration of a dose of the drug.
- AUC is commonly used to assess the extent of drug absorption, distribution, metabolism, and elimination (ADME) within the body.

2. **Calculation**:
- AUC is calculated by integrating the concentration-time curve obtained from plasma drug concentration measurements over a specified time period.
- It can be determined using mathematical methods such as the trapezoidal rule for discrete data points or by fitting a curve to continuous data.

3. **Interpretation**:
- A higher AUC value indicates greater drug exposure and longer duration of action.
- AUC reflects the cumulative effect of absorption, distribution, metabolism, and elimination processes on the drug concentration in the body.
- Changes in AUC can be indicative of alterations in drug absorption, bioavailability, clearance, or drug-drug interactions.

4. **Clinical Significance**:
- AUC is an essential pharmacokinetic parameter used in drug development, dosage regimen optimization, therapeutic drug monitoring, and assessing drug safety and efficacy.
- It helps clinicians and researchers understand and predict drug concentrations in plasma and tissues, which can guide dosing decisions and treatment strategies.
- AUC is often compared between different formulations, doses, or patient populations to evaluate drug performance and bioequivalence.

In summary, the area under the plasma drug concentration-time curve (AUC) provides valuable information about the overall exposure of the body to a drug following administration, playing a crucial role in pharmacokinetic and pharmacodynamic assessments in clinical practice and research.

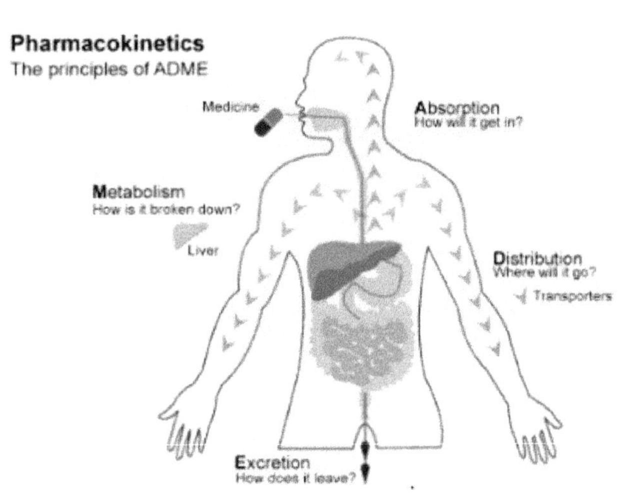

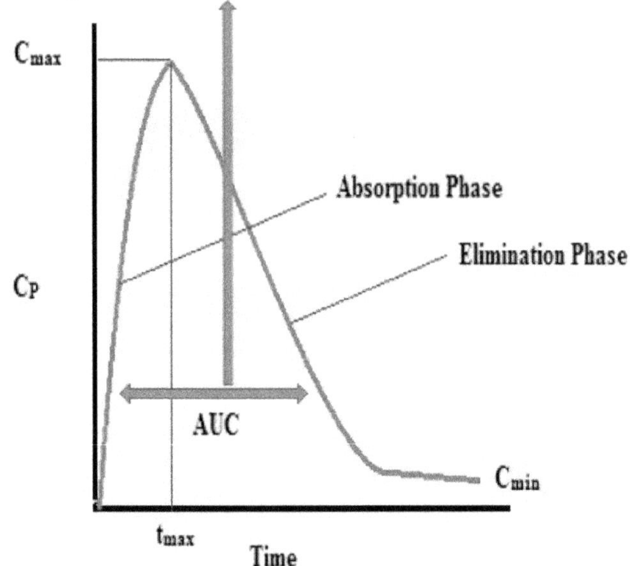

Timepoint (Ti)	Aval (Yi)	Ti – Ti-1	Absolute (Yi +Yi-1)/2	(Ti-Ti-1) X (Yi +Yi-1)/2	Sum	AUC= Sum/total time interval
0	10					
60	15	60	25/2=12.5	60 X 12.5 = 750	3060	3060/(180-0)= 17
120	22	60	37/2=18.5	1110		
180	18	60	40/2=20	1200		

MERGE statement has more than one data set with repeats of by values

When you encounter the message "*MERGE statement has more than one data set with repeats of BY values,*" it means that there are **duplicate** values of the BY variables in one or more of the datasets being merged. This message is a warning indicating that the resulting merged dataset may not be as expected due to the presence of duplicate values.

Here's how you can handle this situation:

1. **Identify the Duplicate Values**:
- First, identify which BY variables are causing the duplicates and in which dataset(s) they occur.
- Review the values of the BY variables in each dataset to understand why duplicates are present.

2. **Determine the Desired Outcome**:
- Decide how you want to handle the duplicates. Do you want to keep all duplicate observations, or do you want to eliminate them?

3. **Options for Handling Duplicates**:
- If you want to keep all duplicate observations:
- You can use the `DUPKEY` option in the `MERGE` statement to keep duplicate observations in the resulting dataset.
- Alternatively, you can use a data step with a `BY` statement and a `SET` statement to merge the datasets, which will automatically retain duplicate observations.
   - If you want to eliminate duplicates:
- You can sort the datasets and use the `NODUPKEY` option in the `MERGE` statement to eliminate duplicates based on the BY variables.
- Another option is to use a data step with a `BY` statement and a `SET` statement, along with the `FIRST.` and `LAST.` automatic variables, to identify and eliminate duplicate observations.

4. **Review and Test**:
- After implementing your chosen approach for handling duplicates, carefully review the resulting merged dataset to ensure it meets your expectations.
- Test your code with sample data to verify that it produces the desired outcome and does not inadvertently remove or retain observations incorrectly.

By following these steps, you can effectively address the "MERGE statement has more than one data set with repeats of BY values" warning and handle duplicates appropriately in your SAS code.

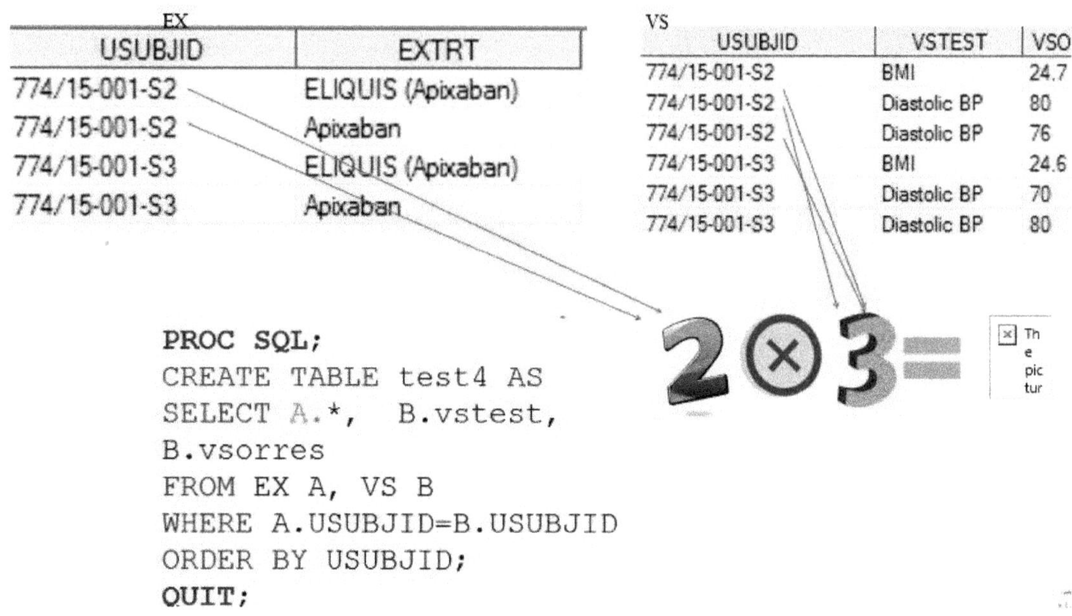

EX	
USUBJID	EXTRT
774/15-001-S2	ELIQUIS (Apixaban)
774/15-001-S2	Apixaban
774/15-001-S3	ELIQUIS (Apixaban)
774/15-001-S3	Apixaban

VS		
USUBJID	VSTEST	VSO
774/15-001-S2	BMI	24.7
774/15-001-S2	Diastolic BP	80
774/15-001-S2	Diastolic BP	76
774/15-001-S3	BMI	24.6
774/15-001-S3	Diastolic BP	70
774/15-001-S3	Diastolic BP	80

```
PROC SQL;
CREATE TABLE test4 AS
SELECT A.*,  B.vstest,
B.vsorres
FROM EX A, VS B
WHERE A.USUBJID=B.USUBJID
ORDER BY USUBJID;
QUIT;
```

Solution Use Proc SQL Many to Many Merge

CHAPTER SIXTY-ONE

Derive BASE,CHG,PCHG AND ABLFL in ADaM LAB (ADLB)

Baseline: Baseline value refers to the *last measurement made prior to administration* of the first dose of study medication.

Change from baseline = post-baseline value – baseline value

USUBJID	LBCAT	LBTESTCD	VISIT	AVAL	LBDT	TRTSDT	flag	ABLFL
101	CHEMISTRY	ALT	SCREENING	13	2018-01-01T09:20:00	2018-01-03T09:01:00	1	
101	CHEMISTRY	ALT	DAY1	15	2018-01-03T09:00:00	2018-01-03T09:01:00	1	Y
101	CHEMISTRY	ALT	WEEK1	10	2018-01-08T09:10:00	2018-01-03T09:01:00	0	
101	CHEMISTRY	ALT	WEEK2	12	2018-01-15T09:07:00	2018-01-03T09:01:00	0	
101	CHEMISTRY	ALT	WEEK4	19	2018-01-29T09:05:00	2018-01-03T09:01:00	0	
101	HEMATOLOGY	BASO	SCREENING	1	2018-01-01T09:20:00	2018-01-03T09:01:00	1	
101	HEMATOLOGY	BASO	DAY1	2	2018-01-03T09:00:00	2018-01-03T09:01:00	1	Y
101	HEMATOLOGY	BASO	WEEK1	1.2	2018-01-08T09:10:00	2018-01-03T09:01:00	0	
101	HEMATOLOGY	BASO	WEEK2	1.1	2018-01-15T09:07:00	2018-01-03T09:01:00	0	
101	HEMATOLOGY	BASO	WEEK4	1	2018-01-29T09:05:00	2018-01-03T09:01:00	0	
101	HEMATOLOGY	WBC	SCREENING	3	2018-01-01T09:00:00	2018-01-03T09:01:00	1	Y
101	HEMATOLOGY	WBC	DAY1	.	2018-01-03T09:00:00	2018-01-03T09:01:00	0	
101	HEMATOLOGY	WBC	WEEK1	3.6	2018-01-08T09:05:00	2018-01-03T09:01:00	0	
101	HEMATOLOGY	WBC	WEEK2	4.1	2018-01-15T09:08:00	2018-01-03T09:01:00	0	
101	HEMATOLOGY	WBC	WEEK4	4.2	2018-01-29T09:09:00	2018-01-03T09:01:00	0	
102	HEMATOLOGY	BASO	SCREENING	.	2018-01-01T09:20:00	2018-01-03T09:01:00	0	
102	HEMATOLOGY	BASO	DAY1	.	2018-01-03T09:00:00	2018-01-03T09:01:00	0	
102	HEMATOLOGY	BASO	WEEK1	1.2	2018-01-08T09:10:00	2018-01-03T09:01:00	0	
102	HEMATOLOGY	BASO	WEEK2	1.1	2018-01-15T09:07:00	2018-01-03T09:01:00	0	
102	HEMATOLOGY	BASO	WEEK4	1	2018-01-29T09:05:00	2018-01-03T09:01:00	0	
102	HEMATOLOGY	WBC	SCREENING	6	2018-01-01T09:00:00	2018-01-03T09:01:00	1	
102	HEMATOLOGY	WBC	DAY1	2	2018-01-03T09:00:00	2018-01-03T09:01:00	1	Y
102	HEMATOLOGY	WBC	WEEK1	3.6	2018-01-08T09:05:00	2018-01-03T09:01:00	0	
102	HEMATOLOGY	WBC	WEEK2	.	2018-01-15T09:08:00	2018-01-03T09:01:00	0	
102	HEMATOLOGY	WBC	WEEK4	4.2	2018-01-29T09:09:00	2018-01-03T09:01:00	0	

ABLFL

USUBJID	LBCAT	LBTESTCD	VISIT	LBDT	TRTSDT	ABLFL	AVAL	BASE	CHG	PCHG
101	CHEMISTRY	ALT	SCREENING	2018-01-01T09:20:00	2018-01-03T09:01:00		13	.	.	.
101	CHEMISTRY	ALT	DAY1	2018-01-03T09:00:00	2018-01-03T09:01:00	Y	15	15	.	.
101	CHEMISTRY	ALT	WEEK1	2018-01-08T09:10:00	2018-01-03T09:01:00		10	15	-5	-33.33
101	CHEMISTRY	ALT	WEEK2	2018-01-15T09:07:00	2018-01-03T09:01:00		12	15	-3	-20
101	CHEMISTRY	ALT	WEEK4	2018-01-29T09:05:00	2018-01-03T09:01:00		19	15	4	26.667
101	HEMATOLOGY	BASO	SCREENING	2018-01-01T09:20:00	2018-01-03T09:01:00		1	.	.	.
101	HEMATOLOGY	BASO	DAY1	2018-01-03T09:00:00	2018-01-03T09:01:00	Y	2	2	.	.
101	HEMATOLOGY	BASO	WEEK1	2018-01-08T09:10:00	2018-01-03T09:01:00		1.2	2	-0.8	-40
101	HEMATOLOGY	BASO	WEEK2	2018-01-15T09:07:00	2018-01-03T09:01:00		1.1	2	-0.9	-45
101	HEMATOLOGY	BASO	WEEK4	2018-01-29T09:05:00	2018-01-03T09:01:00		1	2	-1	-50
101	HEMATOLOGY	WBC	SCREENING	2018-01-01T09:00:00	2018-01-03T09:01:00	Y	9	9	.	.
101	HEMATOLOGY	WBC	DAY1	2018-01-03T09:00:00	2018-01-03T09:01:00		.	9	.	.
101	HEMATOLOGY	WBC	WEEK1	2018-01-08T09:05:00	2018-01-03T09:01:00		3.6	9	-5.4	-60
101	HEMATOLOGY	WBC	WEEK2	2018-01-15T09:08:00	2018-01-03T09:01:00		4.1	9	-4.9	-54.44
101	HEMATOLOGY	WBC	WEEK4	2018-01-29T09:09:00	2018-01-03T09:01:00		4.2	9	-4.8	-53.33
102	HEMATOLOGY	BASO	SCREENING	2018-01-01T09:20:00	2018-01-03T09:01:00		.	.	.	.
102	HEMATOLOGY	BASO	DAY1	2018-01-03T09:00:00	2018-01-03T09:01:00		.	.	.	.
102	HEMATOLOGY	BASO	WEEK1	2018-01-08T09:10:00	2018-01-03T09:01:00		1.2	.	.	.
102	HEMATOLOGY	BASO	WEEK2	2018-01-15T09:07:00	2018-01-03T09:01:00		1.1	.	.	.
102	HEMATOLOGY	BASO	WEEK4	2018-01-29T09:05:00	2018-01-03T09:01:00		1	.	.	.
102	HEMATOLOGY	WBC	SCREENING	2018-01-01T09:00:00	2018-01-03T09:01:00		6	.	.	.
102	HEMATOLOGY	WBC	DAY1	2018-01-03T09:00:00	2018-01-03T09:01:00	Y	2	2	.	.
102	HEMATOLOGY	WBC	WEEK1	2018-01-08T09:05:00	2018-01-03T09:01:00		3.6	2	1.6	80
102	HEMATOLOGY	WBC	WEEK2	2018-01-15T09:08:00	2018-01-03T09:01:00		.	2	.	.
102	HEMATOLOGY	WBC	WEEK4	2018-01-29T09:09:00	2018-01-03T09:01:00		4.2	2	2.2	110

BASE CHG PCHG

CHAPTER SIXTY-TWO

Lab Toxicity Grading ?? Adverse Event Toxicity Grading ??

The National Cancer Institute Common Terminology Criteria, Version 4.0 for Adverse Events (NCI CTCAE) is a descriptive terminology which can be utilized for Adverse Event (AE) reporting (including an abnormal laboratory finding).

ØCommon Terminology Criteria for Adverse Events v4.0 (CTCAE)

ØGrade refers to the severity of the AE.

ØThe CTCAE displays Grades 1 through 5 with unique clinical descriptions of severity for each AE based on this general guideline:

1. **CTCAE**: The Common Terminology Criteria for Adverse Events (CTCAE) is a standardized tool for reporting adverse events in medical settings.

2. **Grading**: Adverse events are graded on a scale of 1 to 5, indicating their severity.

3. **Clinical Descriptions**: Each grade comes with specific clinical descriptions to help categorize the severity level.

4. **Guideline**: The grading is based on a general guideline provided by CTCAE, ensuring consistent interpretation.

5. **Laboratory Findings**: It can also be used to report abnormal laboratory findings, providing a comprehensive framework for assessment.

EGRNCI	Extreme NCI CTCAE Grade	1 = 1	AE.AETOXGR
		2 = 2	
		3 = 3	
		4 = 4	
		5 = 5	

Grades

Grade refers to the severity of the AE. The CTCAE v3.0 displays Grades 1 through 5 with unique clinical descriptions of severity for each AE based on this general guideline:

Grade 1	Mild AE
Grade 2	Moderate AE
Grade 3	Severe AE
Grade 4	Life-threatening or disabling AE
Grade 5	Death related to AE

CTCAE v4.0 Term	Grade 1	Grade 2	Grade 3	Grade 4
Hypercalcemia	>ULN - 11.5 mg/dL; >ULN - 2.9 mmol/L; Ionized calcium >ULN - 1.5 mmol/L	>11.5 - 12.5 mg/dL ; >2.9 - 3.1 mmol/L; Ionized calcium >1.5 - 1.6 mmol/L; symptomatic	>12.5 - 13.5 mg/dL ; >3.1 - 3.4 mmol/L; Ionized calcium >1.6 - 1.8 mmol/L; hospitalization indicated	>13.5 mg/dL; >3.4 mmol/L; Ionized calcium >1.8 mmol/L; life-threatening consequences
Hypocalcemia	<LLN - 8.0 mg/dL; <LLN - 2.0 mmol/L; Ionized calcium <LLN - 1.0 mmol/L	<8.0 - 7.0 mg/dL; <2.0 - 1.75 mmol/L ; Ionized calcium <1.0 - 0.9 mmol/L; symptomatic	<7.0 - 6.0 mg/dL; <1.75 - 1.5 mmol/L; Ionized calcium <0.9 - 0.8 mmol/L; hospitalization indicated	<6.0 mg/dL; <1.5 mmol/L; Ionized calcium <0.8 mmol/L; life-threatening consequences

ULN (Upper Limit of Normal)
LLN (Lower Limit of Normal)

CHAPTER SIXTY-THREE

What are some good programming practices to follow in SAS clinical programming?

1. **Use Meaningful Variable Names:**
   - Choose descriptive and intuitive names for variables to enhance code readability.
   - Avoid generic names like "var1" or "data1" and use names that convey the variable's purpose or content.
2. **Document Your Code:**
   - Include comments to explain the purpose of your code, data manipulation steps, and any assumptions made.
   - Clear documentation facilitates collaboration, code understanding, and troubleshooting.
3. **Follow Coding Standards:**
   - Adhere to coding conventions and standards established by your organization or industry.
   - Consistency in coding style improves code maintainability and readability across projects.
4. **Modularize Your Code:**
   - Break down complex tasks into smaller, manageable modules or functions.
   - Modularization promotes code reuse, simplifies debugging, and enhances scalability.
5. **Validate Input Data:**
   - Verify the integrity and quality of input data by performing data checks.
   - Check for missing values, outliers, or inconsistencies before proceeding with analysis.
6. **Handle Errors Gracefully:**
   - Implement error handling mechanisms to anticipate and manage runtime errors or unexpected conditions.
   - Utilize SAS error-checking techniques like IF-THEN statements and conditional processing.
7. **Optimize Code Performance:**
   - Write efficient code by minimizing redundant calculations and optimizing data processing steps.
   - Utilize appropriate SAS procedures and functions to improve code performance.
8. **Test Your Code:**
   - Thoroughly test your programs under different scenarios and datasets to verify correctness.
   - Use sample data or simulation techniques for testing to identify potential issues early.
9. **Version Control:**
   - Use version control systems like Git to manage code versions, track changes, and collaborate effectively.
   - Version control helps maintain a history of code modifications and facilitates code review processes.
10. **Documentation and Reporting:**
   - Document analysis methodologies, assumptions, and results comprehensively in analysis reports or documentation.
   - Clearly communicate findings, interpretations, and recommendations to stakeholders for transparency and reproducibility.

Comments (CO) SDTM

The Comments dataset captures comments from two distinct sources:

1. **Topical Case Report Form (CRF) Pages**: Comments collected alongside other data on specific CRF pages, such as those related to Adverse Events. These comments are integrated into the relevant sections of the CRF.

2. **Dedicated Comments Page**: Comments gathered on a separate page dedicated solely to capturing comments. This page serves as a centralized repository for comments not tied to any specific data field or form, providing a comprehensive overview of additional remarks or observations.

The CODTC (Date/Time of Comment) field in the dataset adheres to the ISO 8601 standard, specifying the timing of comments made on the dedicated comment form. This field should be null under two conditions:

1. If the comment is a child record of another domain, meaning it's associated with another dataset or form.

2. If the comment date/time was not collected, indicating that no specific timestamp was recorded for the comment.

CHAPTER SIXTY-FIVE

Time-To-Event Data Analysis overall survival rate Summary

Time-to-event data analysis, often used in medical research, assesses the time it takes for an event of interest to occur, such as patient survival or disease progression. When analyzing overall survival rates, several key summary measures are commonly reported:

Overall Survival (OS): The length of time from either the date of diagnosis or the start of treatment for a disease to the date of death from any cause. In clinical trials, it's a common endpoint used to measure the effectiveness of treatments.

Median Survival Time: The time point at which half of the patients have experienced the event of interest (e.g., death). It provides a measure of central tendency for survival times.

Survival Rates at Specific Time Points: These rates indicate the proportion of patients who have not experienced the event of interest (e.g., death) at specific time intervals, such as 1 year, 3 years, or 5 years post-treatment.

Kaplan-Meier Curves: Graphical representation of survival probabilities over time, illustrating the proportion of patients surviving at each time point.

Hazard Ratios: Measure the relative risk of experiencing the event of interest between different groups (e.g., treatment vs. control), after adjusting for other factors.

Log-Rank Test: Statistical test used to compare survival curves between different groups, assessing whether there are significant differences in survival rates.

Cox Proportional Hazards Model: Statistical model used to analyze the effect of multiple factors (e.g., treatment, age, gender) on survival time while adjusting for covariates.

These summary measures provide insights into the overall survival experience of patients in a study population and help researchers and clinicians evaluate the effectiveness of treatments and identify factors influencing survival outcomes.

Observations are called censored when the information about their survival time is incomplete; the most commonly encountered form is right censoring.

CHAPTER SIXTY-SIX

SAS Macro Functions

1) %BQUOTE allows macro variable values to be generated during macro execution, %NRBQUOTE suppresses macro quoting for macro-generated text, and %SUPERQ retrieves the value of a macro variable without resolving its value.

2) %EVAL calculates arithmetic expressions, while %SYSEVALF evaluates arithmetic and logical expressions, returning floating-point results.

3) %INDEX searches for a substring within a larger string and returns the position of its first occurrence.

4) %LENGTH returns the length of a character string or the number of elements in an array.

5) %QUOTE masks special characters in a macro variable for later use, %NRQUOTE temporarily disables macro quoting.

6) SCAN extracts words from a character string, %SCAN operates on macro variables, and %QSCAN treats special characters as literal text.

7) %STR defines a string of text within a macro, while %NRSTR disables macro quoting for the enclosed text.

8) SUBSTR extracts substrings from a larger string, %SUBSTR operates on macro variables, and %QSUBSTR treats special characters as literal text.

9) %SYSFUNC executes a SAS function within a macro, %QSYSFUNC masks special characters in function arguments.

10) %SYSGET retrieves the value of a SAS system option or environment variable.

11) %SYSPROD returns the product release number for the current SAS session.

12) %UNQUOTE resolves macro quoting for a character string, allowing special characters to be interpreted.

13) UPCASE converts a string to uppercase, %UPCASE operates on macro variables, and %QUPCASE treats special characters as literal text.

Proc transpose without out= statement ???

Name	Subject	Marks
Samma	Maths	96
Sandy	English	76
Devesh	German	76
Rakesh	Maths	50
Priya	English	62
Kranti	Maths	92
William	German	87

```
proc transpose data = transp ;
id name;
run;
```

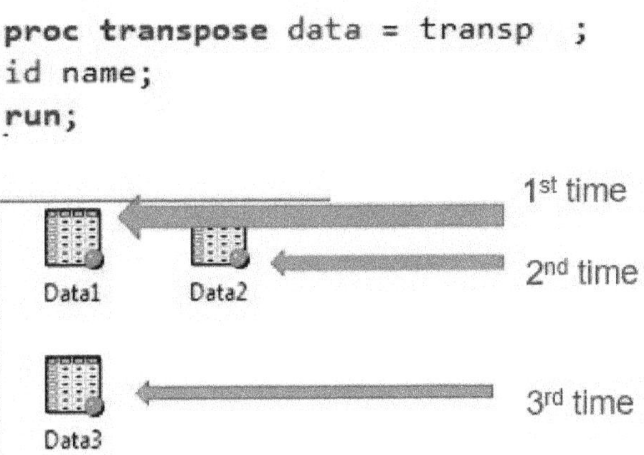

CHAPTER SIXTY-EIGHT

Proc sort without by statement ???

```
proc sort data=transp out=sortt ;run;
```

```
40    proc sort data=transp out=sortt ;run;

ERROR: No BY statement used or no BY variables specified. A BY statement must be used with
       variable names to sort on.
NOTE: The SAS System stopped processing this step because of errors.
WARNING: The data set WORK.SORTT may be incomplete.  When this step was stopped there were 0
         observations and 0 variables.
WARNING: Data set WORK.SORTT was not replaced because this step was stopped.
NOTE: PROCEDURE SORT used (Total process time):
```

CHAPTER SIXTY-NINE

The difference between BY and CLASS ???

The BY statement **repeats** an analysis on every subgroup. The subgroups are treated as independent samples.

The CLASS statement includes a categorical variable as part of an analysis. Often the CLASS variable is used to **compare the groups**, such as in a *t* test or an ANOVA analysis.

Using the BY statement is similar to using the CLASS statement and the NWAY option in that PROC MEANS summarizes each BY group as an independent subset of the input data. Therefore, no overall summarization of the input data is available. However, unlike the CLASS statement, the BY statement requires that you **previously sort BY variables.**

```
proc summary data=transp;
      by name;
      var Marks;
      output out=classby1 sum=;
run;


proc summary data=transp;
      class name;
      var Marks;
      output out=classby2 sum=;
run;
```

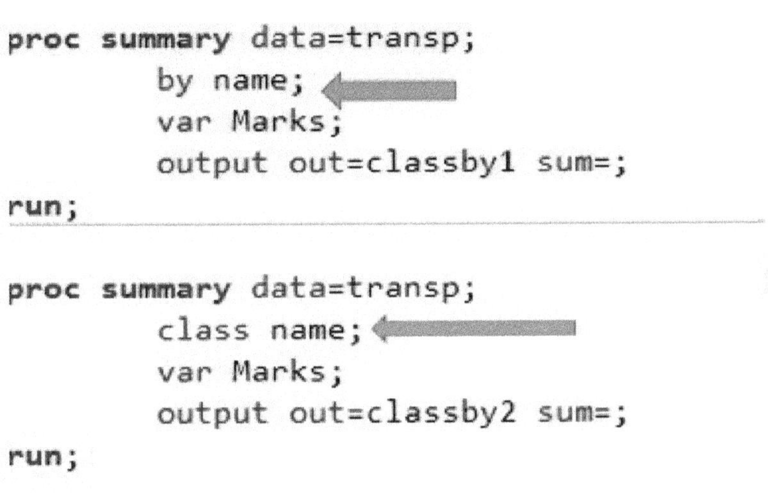

SEE: Work.Classby1

Name	_TYPE_	_FREQ_	Marks
Devesh	0	1	76
Kranti	0	1	92
Priya	0	1	62
Rakesh	0	1	50
Samma	0	1	96
Sandy	0	1	76
William	0	1	87

TABLE: Work.Classby2

Name	_TYPE_	_FREQ_	Marks
	0	7	539
Devesh	1	1	76
Kranti	1	1	92
Priya	1	1	62
Rakesh	1	1	50
Samma	1	1	96
Sandy	1	1	76
William	1	1	87

What s the summary statistics if only 1 subject ???

Graze Type	_TYPE_	_FREQ_	_STAT_	WtGain
continuous	0	1	N	1
continuous	0	1	MIN	12
continuous	0	1	MAX	12
continuous	0	1	MEAN	12
continuous	0	1	STD	.

CHAPTER SEVENTY-ONE

How to extract 2nd word form each row ???

```
data x;
input var $ 1-60 ;
cards;
123 4444 1222 1111 11111 333 4 4444
33333 444 222 111 4444  1111  4 4 44              444
22 44 33 777777 000000 99  8888 777  99999999 00 00
;
run;


data yy;
set x;
nvar=scan (var,-2);
run;
```

	var	nvar
1	123 4444 1222 1111 11111 333 4 4444	4
2	33333 444 222 111 4444 1111 4 4 44 444	44
3	22 44 33 777777 000000 99 8888 777 99999999 00 00	00

CHAPTER SEVENTY-TWO

Variable missing in column statement in PROC REPORT ??

```
proc report nowd nocenter;
COLUMN TYPE ;
  define type / order order=data;
  define num / order order=data;
title 'proc report not in the order of the data';
run;
```

```
38    title 'proc report not in the order of the data';
39    run;

WARNING: num is not in the report definition.
NOTE: There were 7 observations read from the data set WORK.NEW.
NOTE: PROCEDURE REPORT used (Total process time):
      real time           0.03 seconds
      cpu time            0.03 seconds
```

How to remove special characters from string? ??

```
data a_;

  x='abëd34Ý90$#$%a';

  new=compress(x,"ABCDEFGHIJKLMNOPQRSTUVWXYZ1234567890`~!@#$%^&*()-_=+\|[]{};:',.<>?/ " , "kis");

run;
```

	x	new
1	abëd34Ý90$#$%a	abd3490$#$%a

Maximum number of title statements ?? incase how to add extra titles?

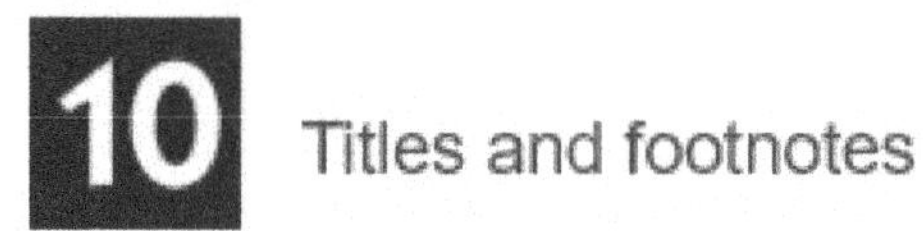

Titles and footnotes

Example 2: Customizing Titles by Using BY Variable Values

You can customize titles by inserting BY variable values in the titles that you specify in PRO

- `title 'Quarterly Sales for #byval(site)';`

- `title 'Annual Costs for #byvar2';`

- `title 'Data Group #byline';`

```
* Text Line using COMPUTE;
title1 'Using Proc REPORT';
title2 'Footnote Using LINE';
proc report data=rptdata.clinics
                (where=(region in('1' '2' '3' '4')
            nowd;
  column region sex wt,(n mean);
  define region / group format=$6.;
  define sex     / group format=$6. 'Gender';
  define wt      / analysis;
  compute after region;
    line ' ';
  endcomp;
  compute after;
    line @20 'Weight taken during';
    line @20 'the entrance exam.';
  endcomp;
  run;
```

```
Using Proc REPORT
Footnote Using LINE

                        weight in pounds
    region  Gender          n        mean
    1       M               4         195

    2       F               6   109.66667
            M               4         105

    3       F               5       127.8
            M               5       163.8

    4       F               4         143
```

How to delete all datasets in work library ??

```
proc datasets lib=work kill memtype=data;
run;
quit;
```

CAUTION:
The KILL option deletes the SAS files immediately after you submit the statement.   [cautionend]

RELREC {Related Records}

Sure, here's a simpler breakdown:

1. **What is RELREC?**
- RELREC is a part of SDTM used to show connections between different records in a clinical trial dataset.

2. **Key Variables:**
- It uses variables like STUDYID (Study Identifier) and USUBJID (Subject Identifier) to identify the study and subjects.
- Other important variables include RDOMAIN (Domain code), IDVAR (Record Identifier), IDVARVAL (Identifier Value), RELTYPE (Type of Relationship), and RELID (Relationship Identifier).

3. **How Relationships are Defined:**
- Each relationship is assigned a unique RELID.
- It links records based on identifiers like AESEQ (Adverse Event Sequence Number) or LBGRPID (Laboratory Group Identifier).

4. **Why it's Useful:**
- RELREC helps researchers understand connections between different types of data collected during a trial.
- For example, it can show if a medication was taken because of an adverse event recorded on a CRF.

5. **Using RELREC:**
- Researchers add records to RELREC for each relationship.
- They use specific variables to specify the type of relationship (ONE or MANY) and identify related records.

6. **Facilitating Analyses:**
- RELREC makes it easier to analyze data by showing how different pieces of information are connected.
- Examples in the paper demonstrate how RELREC can be used for analysis in clinical research.

CHAPTER SEVENTY-SEVEN

Disposition (DS) domain

Here are some simple points based on the provided information:

1. **Purpose of DS Domain:**
- The Disposition (DS) domain records details about subjects enrolled in a study, including key events like informed consent, randomization, completion status, or reasons for discontinuation.

2. **Event Categorization:**
- Events or terms (TERM) in DS are categorized under different criteria known as DSCAT (Disposition Category).
- DSCATs include 'Protocol Milestones', 'Disposition Events', and 'Other Events', each serving a specific purpose in categorizing study events.

3. **Importance of Understanding Criteria:**
- Understanding the differences between DSCAT criteria is crucial for accurately assigning DSCAT values to respective DS terms (DSTERM) or DS decode (DSDECOD).

4. **Study Design Perspective:**
- DS domain captures each subject's unique journey through the study, from enrollment to follow-up and analysis.
- A study's schedule, outlined in the protocol, dictates the timing of various phases and assessments, which are reflected in the DS domain.

5. **Use of CONSORT Flow Diagram:**
- CONSORT flow diagrams, commonly used in clinical trials, visually summarize the stages of the trial from enrollment to analysis.
- Each subject's involvement is depicted from enrollment through follow-up and analysis, with key milestones like informed consent and randomization highlighted.

6. **Enrollment Milestones:**
- Enrollment includes milestones such as 'Signing Informed Consent' and 'Randomization', marking the initiation of screening and allocation processes, respectively.

7. **Subject's Disposition:**
- The subject's disposition reflects their status at various points in the study, including the end of the study.

8. **Illustrative Examples:**
- The subsequent sections provide examples to illustrate how DSCAT values can be assigned based on the study's protocol and flow diagram.

CHAPTER SEVENTY-EIGHT

How to Check Log file or All Log files at a time???

Certainly! You can create a SAS macro to check multiple log files at a time. Here's a simple example of a SAS macro that reads and displays the contents of all log files in a specified directory:

```
%macro check_log_files(directory);
/* Set the directory containing log files */
%let dir = &directory;
    /* Get a list of all log files in the directory */
filename loglist pipe "dir ""&dir.""\*.log /b";
    /* Read and display the contents of each log file */
data _null_;
infile loglist truncover;
input filename $256.;
file print;
filename log "&dir.\&filename";
put "********** Log File: &filename **********";
infile log;
input;
put _infile_;
run;
    /* Close the directory listing */
filename loglist clear;
%mend;
    /* Usage example: Check log files in the directory "C:\Logs" */
%check_log_files(C:\Logs);
```

Here's how the macro works:

1. The macro `%check_log_files` takes one argument, `directory`, which specifies the directory containing the log files to be checked.

2. It uses the `dir` command in a pipe to list all `.log` files in the specified directory.

3. It then reads and displays the contents of each log file using an `infile` statement.

4. The macro closes the directory listing after processing all log files.

You can call this macro with the directory path where your log files are stored. For example, `%check_log_files(C:\Logs)` will check all log files in the directory "C:\Logs".

Feel free to modify the macro according to your specific requirements or preferences. Let me know if you need further assistance!

CHAPTER SEVENTY-NINE

Did you created any Standard macro?? What are the standard macros used in your company???

I haven't developed any standardized macros within our organization, but I have contributed to training new team members on utilizing client-standard macros. Additionally, I've crafted customized macros to streamline repetitive tasks and proposed macro solutions to clients for review and implementation.

Formats
mage
mcpval
mdates
mfreq
mimplab
minop
mlistpg
mnumobs
mpageof
mrelday
msignoff
msplit
mss
mtitle
mtottrt
mwordall
rtdemo2_

Some standard Macros

CHAPTER EIGHTY

How Qc programmer communicate with Primary programmer???

Quality Control (QC) programmers typically communicate with Primary programmers through various channels to ensure smooth collaboration and effective resolution of issues. Here are some common methods:

1. **Email Communication:** QC programmers may directly communicate with Primary programmers via email to discuss project requirements, share updates, report issues, and seek clarification on tasks.

2. **Project Management Tools:** Utilizing project management tools like **JIRA, Tracker, or Prism,** QC programmers can raise tickets or issues, assign them to Primary programmers, track progress, and provide feedback on deliverables.

3. **Regular Meetings:** Scheduled meetings or conference calls allow QC and Primary programmers to discuss project status, address concerns, share insights, and coordinate efforts to meet project deadlines.

4. **Instant Messaging:** Instant messaging platforms like Slack or Microsoft Teams facilitate real-time communication between QC and Primary programmers, enabling quick exchanges of information, updates, and queries.

5. **Documentation:** Maintaining comprehensive project documentation ensures that QC programmers can refer to project specifications, requirements, and guidelines, facilitating clear communication and alignment between teams.

6. **Code Reviews:** QC programmers may conduct code reviews with Primary programmers to assess code quality, identify potential issues or improvements, and ensure adherence to coding standards and best practices.

By leveraging these communication channels and practices, QC programmers and Primary programmers can collaborate effectively, maintain transparency, and deliver high-quality outcomes for projects.

CHAPTER EIGHTY-ONE

Study status sheet

A study status sheet in clinical SAS projects typically provides a summary overview of the current status and progress of the study. Here's what it may include:

1. **Study Information:**
- Study Title
- Study Identifier (Study ID)
- Principal Investigator
- Study Sponsor

2. **Study Timeline:**
- Start Date
- End Date
- Duration

3. **Study Objectives:**
- Brief overview of the study's goals and objectives

4. **Study Milestones:**
- Key milestones achieved (e.g., Protocol Finalization, First Patient First Visit (FPFV), Database Lock, Final Study Report Submission)

5. **Enrollment Status:**
- Total Number of Subjects Enrolled
- Target Enrollment
- Enrollment Rate (e.g., Percentage of Enrollment Achieved)

6. **Data Collection Status:**
- Status of data collection activities (e.g., Case Report Form (CRF) completion, data entry)

7. **Data Cleaning and Quality Control:**
- Status of data cleaning activities
- Quality control metrics (e.g., query status, data discrepancies)

8. **Statistical Analysis Status:**
- Progress of statistical analysis plan implementation
- Completion status of statistical programming tasks

9. **Regulatory Submissions:**
- Status of regulatory submissions (e.g., Investigational New Drug (IND) application, New Drug Application (NDA))

10. **Safety Reporting:**
- Overview of safety reporting activities (e.g., Adverse Events (AEs) reporting, Serious Adverse Events (SAEs) reporting)

11. **Adherence to Timeline:**
- Comparison of actual progress with planned timeline
- Identification of any delays or deviations from the original schedule

12. **Issues and Risks:**
- Identification of any issues, risks, or challenges encountered during the study

- Mitigation strategies implemented or planned to address these issues
    13. **Next Steps:**
- Planned activities and milestones for the upcoming period
- Actions required to address any outstanding issues or risks

The study status sheet serves as a valuable tool for stakeholders to monitor the progress of the study, identify areas needing attention, and make informed decisions to ensure successful study completion.

Entries: xxx: xxx
Location of programs: xxxxxxx\PGM\Listing
Location of outputs: xxxxxxx\Out\Listing

VC – Validation complete (with Statistician) — Senior Stats QC
IQC – Stats QC complete (Ready for Final Review) — Final Stats QC
FQC – Final Stats QC complete (Ready for Delivery to — Client Review

Prgname	Output	OPF	VPF	Comment E	Date Added	Timepoint	Flag	Comment / Finding	Resolution	OP	OP-Dat	VP	VP-Dat
LAE3.SAS	16.2.4.1.1	jaya		jaya	3-Sep-15	Original Release	OC						
LAE3.SAS	16.2.4.1.1			ravi	4-Sep-15	Original Validation	VC	In the footnote "InjP" should be replaced with "Inj&P".	Fixed	shiva	4-Sep-15	ravi	4-Sep-15
LAE3.SAS	16.2.4.1.1					Senior Review							
LAE3.SAS	16.2.4.1.1					Final Stats QC							
LLABS1.SAS	16.2.4.2.1	jaya		jaya	3-Sep-15	Original Release	OC						
LLABS1.SAS	16.2.4.2.1			ravi	4-Sep-15	Original Validation	VC	Instead of 1,2,3,4 in period value you can put Period 1, Period 2, Period 3, Period 4.	Fixed	shiva	4-Sep-15	ravi	4-Sep-15
LLABS1.SAS	16.2.4.2.1					Senior Review							
LLABS1.SAS	16.2.4.2.1					Final Stats QC							
LLABS1.SAS	16.2.4.3.1	jaya		jaya	3-Sep-15	Original Release	OC						
LLABS1.SAS	16.2.4.3.1			ravi	4-Sep-15	Original Validation	VC	No Comment		shiva	4-Sep-15	ravi	4-Sep-15
LLABS1.SAS	16.2.4.3.1					Senior Review							
LLABS1.SAS	16.2.4.3.1					Final Stats QC							
LLABS1.SAS	16.2.4.4.1	jaya		jaya	3-Sep-15	Original Release	OC						
LLABS1.SAS	16.2.4.4.1			ravi	4-Sep-15	Original Validation	VC	Why treatment and period/timepoint is starting from the 2nd row instead of 1st row.	Fixed	shiva	4-Sep-15	ravi	
LLABS1.SAS	16.2.4.4.1					Senior Review							

CHAPTER EIGHTY-TWO

Data issues sheet

A data issues sheet in clinical SAS projects is used to track and manage data-related issues encountered during the course of the study. Here's what it typically includes:

    1. **Issue Identification:**
- Unique Issue ID or Number
- Date when the issue was identified
- Description of the issue

    2. **Data Variable(s) Affected:**
- Names of the variable(s) or dataset(s) impacted by the issue

    3. **Severity Level:**
- Severity rating indicating the impact of the issue on data quality and study outcomes (e.g., Critical, Major, Minor)

    4. **Issue Category:**
- Classification of the issue into categories such as data collection, data entry, data processing, or data analysis

    5. **Root Cause Analysis:**
- Investigation findings and analysis of the root cause(s) leading to the issue

    6. **Impact Assessment:**
- Assessment of the potential impact of the issue on the study results, regulatory submissions, or patient safety

    7. **Resolution Plan:**
- Proposed plan of action to address and resolve the issue
- Assigning responsibility to specific team members for implementing the resolution plan

    8. **Status Tracking:**
- Current status of the issue (e.g., Open, In Progress, Resolved, Closed)
- Target resolution date or timeline for resolution

    9. **Follow-Up Actions:**
- Actions taken or planned to monitor the progress of the resolution plan and ensure the issue is effectively resolved
- Any additional measures implemented to prevent similar issues in the future

    10. **Documentation and Communication:**
- Documentation of all communications and discussions related to the issue, including meeting minutes, emails, or notes
- Communication plan for informing stakeholders about the issue and its resolution progress

    11. **Validation and Verification:**
- Validation activities to ensure that the resolution plan effectively addresses the issue and that data integrity is maintained
- Verification of the resolution outcome to confirm that the issue has been successfully resolved

    12. **Lessons Learned:**
- Lessons learned from addressing the issue, including best practices, recommendations, or process improvements for future studies

    The data issues sheet serves as a centralized repository for tracking, managing, and resolving data-related issues throughout the study lifecycle, helping to ensure data quality and integrity.

ss	Datase	Subject	Data Issues	Issue Da	Programme	Comment	Resolution	Resolved	Resolved Dat
1	AE	01-04'	Spelling mistake in 'Adverse event' Reported term.	########	jaya Baviskar	Spelling mistake in 'Adverse event' Reported term. It is entered as 'BURN (RIGTH HAND)'. Kindly correct the spelling of 'RIGTH' to 'RIGHT'. Thanks.			
2	AE	01-05'	AE sponsor ID not collected as per date occurred.	########	jaya Baviskar	Subject has AESPID as '4' for the Adverse event 'HEADACHE'; for Start date 07JUN2015; however the same subject has AESPID as '5' for the Adverse event 'MENSES CYCLE MORE LONGER THAN USUAL' with a start date as '06JUN2015'. Kindly investigate and address the discrepancy. Thank you.			

CHAPTER EIGHTY-THREE

Hard Coding

Hardcoding consisted of adding one or a few lines of program code in these programs. ... As a result, revalidation of the **SAS** programs is not required, if the values need to be changed.

1. **Definition:**
- Hard coding involves embedding specific values or parameters directly into SAS programs instead of using variables or references.

2. **Purpose:**
- It's used for data manipulation, analysis specifications, and report generation in clinical SAS programming.

3. **Risk of Errors:**
- Hard coding increases the risk of errors as changes to hardcoded values require manual updates throughout the program.

4. **Lack of Flexibility:**
- It limits the flexibility and scalability of SAS programs as they become less adaptable to changes in data or analysis requirements.

5. **Documentation and Reproducibility:**
- Hard coding makes it difficult to document and understand the logic behind the analysis, hindering reproducibility and validation of results.

6. **Best Practices:**
- It's advisable to minimize hard coding and use parameterization and variable referencing for improved maintainability and accuracy of the code.

We engage in hard coding in alignment with client and statistical requirements, ensuring thorough documentation for audit purposes.

	USUBJID		LBSEQ		LBTESTCD		LBTEST		LBSTRESN		LBSTRESU
1	ABC01-012-0067		52		NEUTLE		Neutrophils/Leukocytes		58.7		%
2	ABC01-028-0144		18		NEUTLE		Neutrophils/Leukocytes		0.612		fraction of 1

Table 2. Example LB Dataset

Since all of the NEUTLE fraction results needed to be converted to a percent, and there were only 3 instances of this happening in the clinical data, the programmer used the following code in their LB program:

```
data lbremap;
  set lb;
    if usubjid="ABC01-028-0144" and lbtestcd="NEUTLE" and lbseq=18 then do;
      lbstresn=61.2;
      lbstresu="%";
    end;
  run;
```

CHAPTER EIGHTY-FOUR

Geometric Mean & Mean calculation in SAS

geometric mean calculation.

One of the ways to calculate it is by taking the log of the variable and giving that in VAR statement of proc means.

Calculating the geometric mean by taking the log of the variable and then using it in the VAR statement of PROC MEANS is a common approach. Here's how you can do it using PROC UNIVARIATE:

```
/* Sample data */
data example;
input value;
datalines;
10
20
30
;
    /* Calculate geometric mean using PROC UNIVARIATE */
proc univariate data=example;
var log_value = log(value);
output out=geometric_means mean=geometric_mean;
run;
    /* Display the geometric mean */
proc print data=geometric_means;
var geometric_mean;
run;
```

In this example:

1. We calculate the logarithm of the variable `value` and store it in a new variable `log_value`.

2. We then use `log_value` in the VAR statement of PROC UNIVARIATE.

3. The OUTPUT statement is used to output the mean of the log-transformed variable into a new dataset called `geometric_means`.

4. Finally, we use PROC PRINT to display the calculated geometric mean.

This approach leverages the property that the geometric mean of log-transformed values is equal to the arithmetic mean of the log-transformed values, and then exponentiating this value gives the geometric mean of the original data.

CHAPTER EIGHTY-FIVE

95% confidence interval (CI)

Certainly! Here's a step-by-step guide to manually calculate a 95% confidence interval (CI) in SAS, including definitions for each step:

1. **Sample Mean ($\bar{x}$):**
- Calculate the arithmetic mean of your sample data.
- The sample mean is the average value of all observations in your sample.

2. **Sample Standard Deviation (s):**
- Calculate the standard deviation of your sample data.
- The sample standard deviation measures the dispersion or spread of values in your sample around the mean.

3. **Standard Error of the Mean (SE):**
- Compute the standard error of the mean, which estimates the variability of sample means.
- The standard error of the mean is calculated as the sample standard deviation divided by the square root of the sample size (SE = s / √n).

4. **Critical Value (t*):**
- Determine the critical value from the t-distribution corresponding to the desired confidence level (e.g., 95% confidence level or alpha = 0.05).
- The critical value is used to determine the margin of error and accounts for the uncertainty in estimating the population mean from a sample.

5. **Margin of Error (ME):**
- Calculate the margin of error, which represents the maximum likely difference between the sample mean and the population mean.
- The margin of error is computed as the critical value multiplied by the standard error of the mean (ME = t* * SE).

6. **Confidence Interval (CI):**
- Compute the lower and upper bounds of the confidence interval around the sample mean.
- The confidence interval provides a range of values within which the true population mean is likely to lie.
- The lower bound of the confidence interval is calculated as the sample mean minus the margin of error, while the upper bound is the sample mean plus the margin of error.

Here's an example SAS code snippet demonstrating these steps with the corresponding definitions:

```
/* Sample data */
data example;
input value;
datalines;
10
20
30
;

    /* Calculate mean and standard deviation */
proc means data=example mean std;
```

```
var value;
run;
    /* Store mean and standard deviation in macro variables */
data _null_;
set summary;
if _STAT_ = "MEAN" then do;
call symputx('mean', mean);
call symputx('std_dev', std);
end;
run;
    /* Sample size */
%let n = 3;
    /* Calculate standard error of the mean */
%let se = &std_dev / sqrt(&n);
    /* Calculate critical value from t-distribution (for alpha = 0.05 and df = n - 1) */
%let t_star = %sysfunc(tinv(0.975, &n - 1)); /* For two-tailed test */
    /* Calculate margin of error */
%let me = &t_star * &se;
    /* Calculate confidence interval */
%let lower_bound = &mean - &me;
%let upper_bound = &mean + &me;
    /* Output results */
%put 95% Confidence Interval: (&lower_bound, &upper_bound);
```

This code calculates the 95% confidence interval for the sample data using manual calculations in SAS, including definitions for each step. Adjust the sample data and parameters as needed for your analysis.

CHAPTER EIGHTY-SIX

P-value

1. **P-value Definition:**
- The p-value measures evidence against the null hypothesis in a statistical test.
- It represents the probability of observing a test statistic as extreme as the one observed, assuming the null hypothesis is true.
   2. **Interpretation of P-values:**
- A small p-value (usually < 0.05) indicates significant evidence against the null hypothesis.
- Large p-values suggest results compatible with the null hypothesis.
   3. **Consideration of 95% Confidence Interval (CI):**
- A 95% CI estimates the range of likely values for a population parameter.
- If the 95% CI excludes the null value, it signifies significance at the 0.05 level.

CHAPTER EIGHTY-SEVEN

ADaM IG 1.1 and 1.0 Difference??

Table 1.3.1.1 Other CDISC Documents and their Applicability to ADaMIG Versions

Document	ADaMIG v1.0	ADaMIG v1.1
Analysis Data Model (ADaM) v2.1, December 2009	Foundation document for ADaMIG v1.0	Still applicable
ADaM Examples in Commonly Used Statistical Analysis Methods v1.0, December 2011	Written for ADaMIG v1.0	Still applicable
The ADaM Basic Data Structure for Time-to-Event Analyses v1.0, May 2012	Written for ADaMIG v1.0	Still applicable
Update to the first CDISC SDTM/ADaM Pilot Project, January 2013	Written for ADaMIG v1.0	Still applicable
ADaM Data Structure for Adverse Event Analysis v1.0, May 2012	Written for ADaMIG v1.0	Superseded by OCCDS v1.0
ADaM Structure for Occurrence Data (OCCDS) v1.0, February, 2016	Not written for ADaMIG v1.0	Written for ADaMIG v1.1
CDISC ADaM Validation Checks v1.3, March 2015	Written for ADaMIG v1.0	Mostly applicable; v1.4 will be written for ADaMIG v1.1
Define-XML v2.0, March 2013	Applicable	Applicable
Analysis Results Metadata Specification for Define-XML Version 2 v1.0, January 2015	Applicable	Applicable

Enter Caption

CHAPTER EIGHTY-EIGHT

Automatic date, time, and page numbers

To include automatic date, time, and page numbers in footnotes in SAS, you can use the system macro variables `&sysdate`, `&systime`, and the automatic page number macro variable `&page`. Here's how you can do it:

```
/* Example SAS code */
ods html file='output.html' style=meadow;
    /* Use ODS escapechar to insert dynamic values in footnotes */
ods escapechar='^';
    proc print data=sashelp.class;
run;
    ods html close;
    /* Output footnotes with date, time, and page number */
options nodate nonumber;
ods escapechar='^';
ods html body='output.html' (footnote='^{&sysdate} ^{&systime} Page ^{&page}');
```

In this example:

- `ods escapechar='^';` sets the escape character to `^`, which allows you to reference macro variables within the ODS statement.
- `ods html body='output.html'` specifies the HTML output file and sets the body of the HTML document.
- `footnote='^{&sysdate} ^{&systime} Page ^{&page}'` inserts the system date, system time, and page number into the footnote using macro variable references within curly braces `{}`.
- `options nodate nonumber;` suppresses the default date and page numbers in the output.

Adjust the ODS destination and output format as needed for your specific requirements. This example generates an HTML output file with dynamic date, time, and page numbers included in the footnotes.

CHAPTER EIGHTY-NINE

INDEX function

In SAS, the INDEX function is used to search for a substring within a larger string and returns the position of the first occurrence of the substring. If the substring is not found, the function returns 0. Here's how the INDEX function works with examples:

```
/* Example 1: Using INDEX function to find substring */
data _null_;
/* Define a string */
string = "Hello, world!";

/* Search for substring "world" within the string */
position = index(string, "world");

/* Print the position of the substring */
put position=;
run;
```

In this example, the INDEX function searches for the substring "world" within the string "Hello, world!". Since "world" is found starting from position 8 in the string, the function returns the value 8.

```
/* Example 2: Using INDEX function when substring is not found */
data _null_;
/* Define a string */
string = "Hello, world!";

/* Search for substring "universe" within the string */
position = index(string, "universe");

/* Print the position of the substring */
put position=;
run;
```

In this example, the INDEX function searches for the substring "universe" within the string "Hello, world!". Since "universe" is not found in the string, the function returns 0.

You can use the result of the INDEX function in conditional statements or further processing as needed in your SAS programs.

CHAPTER NINETY

Difference between SDTM SEQ vs ADAM ASEQ??

The main difference between SDTMSEQ and ADaM ASEQ lies in their purpose and usage within clinical data standards:

1. **SDTMSEQ (SDTM Sequence Number):**

- SDTMSEQ is a variable used in SDTM (Study Data Tabulation Model) datasets to denote the order of occurrence of records within a subject.

- It is typically used to maintain the chronological order of records, such as events, findings, or interventions, within SDTM domains.

- SDTMSEQ facilitates the organization and analysis of data by ensuring that records are properly sequenced and can be interpreted in the context of time.

2. **ADaM ASEQ (Analysis Sequence Number):**

- ADaM ASEQ is a variable used in ADaM (Analysis Data Model) datasets to denote the order of records within an analysis dataset.

- Unlike SDTMSEQ, which primarily focuses on the chronological order of data collection events, ADaM ASEQ is used to establish the sequence of observations within an analysis dataset.

- ADaM ASEQ facilitates the analysis and interpretation of data by ensuring that observations are properly ordered and can be analyzed in a logical sequence.

In summary, while both SDTMSEQ and ADaM ASEQ involve sequencing records within datasets, they serve different purposes within their respective data standards. SDTMSEQ maintains the order of data collection events in SDTM datasets, whereas ADaM ASEQ establishes the sequence of observations within analysis datasets for statistical analysis and reporting purposes.

In SDTM datasets, even records that are marked as "not done" or otherwise incomplete are typically assigned a sequence number (SDTMSEQ). This ensures that all records, including those with missing or incomplete data, are accounted for and maintain their chronological order within the dataset.

CHAPTER NINETY-ONE

Difference between sevreity and maximum severity ae table

The main difference between "Severity" and "Maximum Severity" in adverse event (AE) tables lies in their definitions and how they are captured:

    1. **Severity:**

- Severity refers to the degree of intensity or seriousness of an adverse event experienced by a subject.

- It is typically assessed and recorded by the investigator or healthcare professional based on clinical judgment and predefined criteria.

- Severity levels often include categories such as mild, moderate, severe, and life-threatening, indicating the extent of impact or harm caused by the adverse event.

    2. **Maximum Severity:**

- Maximum Severity represents the **most severe level** of intensity observed for a specific adverse event across all occurrences for a subject.

- It is determined by evaluating the severity of each occurrence of the adverse event and selecting the highest severity level recorded.

- Maximum Severity provides a summary measure of the most significant impact of an adverse event on a subject throughout the study period.

In summary, while Severity captures the intensity of individual occurrences of adverse events, Maximum Severity summarizes the overall severity of an adverse event by considering the most severe occurrence recorded for each subject. Both measures are important for understanding the clinical significance and impact of adverse events in clinical trials.

CHAPTER NINETY-TWO

How can you filter only numeric variables from dataset ?

In SAS, you can filter only numeric variables from a dataset using PROC CONTENTS or the dictionary tables. Here's how you can do it:

Using PROC CONTENTS:

```
/* Use PROC CONTENTS to list variable information */
proc contents data=your_dataset out=var_info(keep=name type) noprint;
run;
    /* Filter only numeric variables */
data numeric_vars;
set var_info;
where type = 1; /* Type 1 indicates numeric variables */
run;
```

Using Dictionary Tables:

```
/* Create a dataset containing variable information from DICTIONARY.TABLES */
proc sql noprint;
create table var_info as
select libname, memname, name, type
from dictionary.columns
where libname = 'YOUR_LIBRARY_NAME' /* Replace with your library name */
and memname = 'YOUR_DATASET_NAME' /* Replace with your dataset name */
and type = 'num';
quit;
```

In these examples:

- PROC CONTENTS is used to extract variable information from the dataset, and the TYPE variable is used to identify numeric variables (TYPE=1).

- The DICTIONARY.COLUMNS table is queried using PROC SQL, and the TYPE variable is filtered for numeric variables ('num').

After filtering, you'll have a dataset (numeric_vars or var_info) containing only the numeric variables from your original dataset. Adjust the dataset and library names as needed for your specific dataset.

CHAPTER NINETY-THREE

How can you count number of observations in dataset??

To count the number of observations in a dataset using PROC SQL, you can use the COUNT function. Here's how you can do it:

/* Using PROC SQL to count observations */
proc sql noprint;
select count(*) as num_obs
from your_dataset; /* Replace with your dataset name */
quit;
    In this example:
    - The SELECT statement retrieves the count of observations from the dataset specified in the FROM clause.
- The COUNT(*) function counts all observations in the dataset.
- The AS keyword is used to rename the count to num_obs.
    After executing this PROC SQL step, the result will be a table with a single row containing the count of observations in your dataset under the column named num_obs.

CHAPTER NINETY-FOUR

Ecg parameter names?

In ADaM (Analysis Data Model) datasets for ECG (Electrocardiogram) parameters, common variable names typically correspond to specific ECG measurements or intervals. Here are some examples of commonly used ECG parameter names in ADaM datasets:

1. **ECG Parameter Names:**
- **QT Interval:** QT, QTc, QT_CORRECTED
- **RR Interval:** RR, RR_INTERVAL
- **PR Interval:** PR, PR_INTERVAL
- **QRS Duration:** QRS, QRS_DURATION
- **Heart Rate:** HR, HEART_RATE
- **ST Segment:** ST_SEGMENT
- **P Wave:** P_WAVE_AMPLITUDE, P_WAVE_DURATION
- **T Wave:** T_WAVE_AMPLITUDE, T_WAVE_DURATION
- **ECG Lead:** LEAD_I, LEAD_II, LEAD_III, LEAD_AVR, LEAD_AVL, LEAD_AVF, LEAD_V1, LEAD_V2, LEAD_V3, LEAD_V4, LEAD_V5, LEAD_V6

These variable names may vary depending on the specific analysis requirements and conventions used by individual organizations or studies. It's essential to consult the data specifications or documentation provided with the dataset to understand the exact variable names and their meanings in the context of your analysis.

Certainly! Here are additional derived ECG parameter names commonly found in ADaM datasets:

1. Heart Rate Acceleration (HRA)
2. Heart Rate Deceleration (HRD)
3. Heart Rate Turbulence Slope (HRTS)
4. Deceleration Capacity (DC)
5. QT Interval Variability (QTV)
6. QT Interval Dispersion (QTD)
7. Signal Quality Index (SQI)
8. Noise Level (NL)
9. Signal-to-Noise Ratio (SNR)
10. Low Frequency (LF)
11. High Frequency (HF)
12. LF/HF Ratio
13. P Wave Axis (PAX)
14. P Wave Area (PWA)
15. T Wave Axis (TAX)
16. T Wave Amplitude (TWA)
17. QRS Axis (QAX)
18. QRS Amplitude (QRSA)
19. Mean RR Interval
20. Root Mean Square of Successive Differences (RMSSD)

21. ST Segment Elevation (STE)
22. ST Segment Depression (STD)
23. ST Segment Slope (STS)

These derived parameters provide detailed insights into cardiac function, rhythm, and variability, contributing to comprehensive analyses in clinical research.

CHAPTER NINETY-FIVE

DV DVTERM or SDTM variable MORE THAN 200 Length??

- SAS v5 Transport file format limits storage for long text strings.
- SDTMIG defines conventions for storing long text strings using multiple variables.
- For general-observation-class variables and supplemental qualifiers:
- **First 200 characters stored in parent domain variable.**
- **Additional 200 characters stored in SUPP-- dataset.**
- Text split between words for readability.
- QNAM describes non-standard variable without numeric suffix.
- QNAM for additional text contains sequential variable name.
- QLABEL is original domain variable label.
- Label suffix not appended for long text strings to maintain concept.
- Conceptually different from storing multiple values for a single variable.
- Unique naming required for QNAM and QLABEL for multiple values.
- For standard domain names already 8 characters long, replace last character with a digit for QNAM values.

CHAPTER NINETY-SIX

Therapeutic areas of clinical research

- Cardiology: Focuses on the study and treatment of heart diseases and disorders.
- Oncology: Concentrates on the diagnosis and treatment of cancer.
- Gastroenterology: Specializes in digestive system disorders.
- Neurology: Deals with disorders of the nervous system.
- Psychiatry: Focuses on mental health disorders and treatments.
- Infectious Diseases: Concentrates on illnesses caused by pathogens.
- Endocrinology: Specializes in hormone-related disorders.
- Rheumatology: Focuses on disorders of the joints, muscles, and connective tissues.
- Pulmonology: Concentrates on diseases of the respiratory system.
- Nephrology: Specializes in kidney diseases and disorders.
- Dermatology: Focuses on skin disorders and treatments.
- Hematology: Concentrates on diseases of the blood and blood-forming organs.
- Ophthalmology: Specializes in eye disorders and treatments.
- Immunology: Focuses on the study of the immune system and its disorders.
- Obstetrics and Gynecology: Concentrates on women's reproductive health.
- Pediatrics: Specializes in the medical care of children.
- Geriatrics: Focuses on the medical care of elderly individuals.

CHAPTER NINETY-SEVEN

Controlled terminology

Controlled Terminology is the set of codelists and valid values used with data items within CDISC-defined datasets.

Controlled Terminology provides the values required for submission to FDA and PMDA in CDISC-compliant datasets.

Controlled Terminology does not tell you *WHAT* to collect; it tells you *IF* you collected a particular data item, how you should submit it in your electronic dataset.

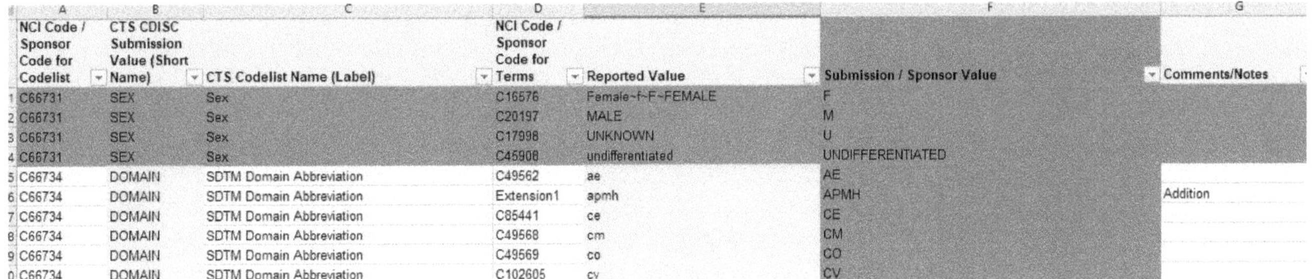

	NCI Code / Sponsor Code for Codelist	CTS CDISC Submission Value (Short Name)	CTS Codelist Name (Label)	NCI Code / Sponsor Code for Terms	Reported Value	Submission / Sponsor Value	Comments/Notes
1	C66731	SEX	Sex	C16576	Female~f~F~FEMALE	F	
2	C66731	SEX	Sex	C20197	MALE	M	
3	C66731	SEX	Sex	C17998	UNKNOWN	U	
4	C66731	SEX	Sex	C45908	undifferentiated	UNDIFFERENTIATED	
5	C66734	DOMAIN	SDTM Domain Abbreviation	C49562	ae	AE	
6	C66734	DOMAIN	SDTM Domain Abbreviation	Extension1	apmh	APMH	Addition
7	C66734	DOMAIN	SDTM Domain Abbreviation	C85441	ce	CE	
8	C66734	DOMAIN	SDTM Domain Abbreviation	C49568	cm	CM	
9	C66734	DOMAIN	SDTM Domain Abbreviation	C49569	co	CO	
0	C66734	DOMAIN	SDTM Domain Abbreviation	C102605	cv	CV	

CONTROLLED TERMINOLOGY SHEET CDISC

CHAPTER NINETY-EIGHT

Compliance(%)

The formula to calculate Compliance (%) in Clinical SAS is:

Compliance (%)=(Total Planned Activities/Total Planned Activities Taken)×100

Where:

- Total Planned Activities Taken: The total number of activities completed or taken as per the study protocol.
- Total Planned Activities: The total number of activities planned or specified in the study protocol.

CHAPTER NINETY-NINE

Concomitant Medications Indicator Variables

Table 3.2.5.4 Concomitant Medications Indicator Variables

Variable Name	Variable Label	Type	Code List / Controlled Terms	Core	CDISC Notes
ONTRTFL	On Treatment Record Flag	Char	Y	Cond	Character indicator of whether the observation occurred while the subject was on treatment. Example derivation: If ADSL.TRTSDT <= ASTDT <= ADSL.TRTEDT then ONTRTFL = 'Y' This variable is conditional on whether the concept of on-treatment is a feature of the study and used in analysis.

Pre-treatment Flag & Follow-up Flag

Variable Name	Variable Label	Type	Code List / Controlled Terms	Core	CDISC Notes
PREFL	Pre-treatment Flag	Char	Y	Cond	Character indicator of whether the observation occurred before the subject started treatment. Example derivation: If ASTDT < ADSL.TRTSDT then PREFL='Y' This variable is conditional on whether the concept of pre-treatment is a feature of the study and used in analysis.
FUPFL	Follow-up Flag	Char	Y	Cond	Character indicator of whether the observation occurred while the subject was on follow-up. Example derivation: If ASTDT > ADSL.TRTEDT then FUPFL='Y' This variable is conditional on whether the concept of follow-up is a feature of the study and used in analysis.

Enter Caption

ECG CS & NCS??

1. **ECG CS (Clinical Significance)**: Refers to the core segment of an electrocardiogram (ECG) signal containing standard waveform components essential for diagnosing clinically significant cardiac abnormalities, such as arrhythmias, ischemia, and conduction disturbances.

2. **ECG NCS (Non-Clinical Significance)**: Encompasses non-core segments of the ECG signal that, while not directly indicative of clinically significant cardiac conditions, may provide additional information or context. These segments could include variations in heart rate, minor waveform abnormalities, or artifacts that are not indicative of pathology.

3. **Purpose**: Distinguishing between ECG CS and NCS aids in focusing clinical attention on critical waveform components while acknowledging and interpreting non-core segments for a comprehensive assessment of cardiac health.

"ECG CS & NCS" differentiates between the core segment (CS), containing essential waveform components for diagnosing cardiac abnormalities, and the non-core segment (NCS), which includes supplementary data that may not directly indicate pathology but provides additional context for cardiac assessment.

Core variables in SDTM

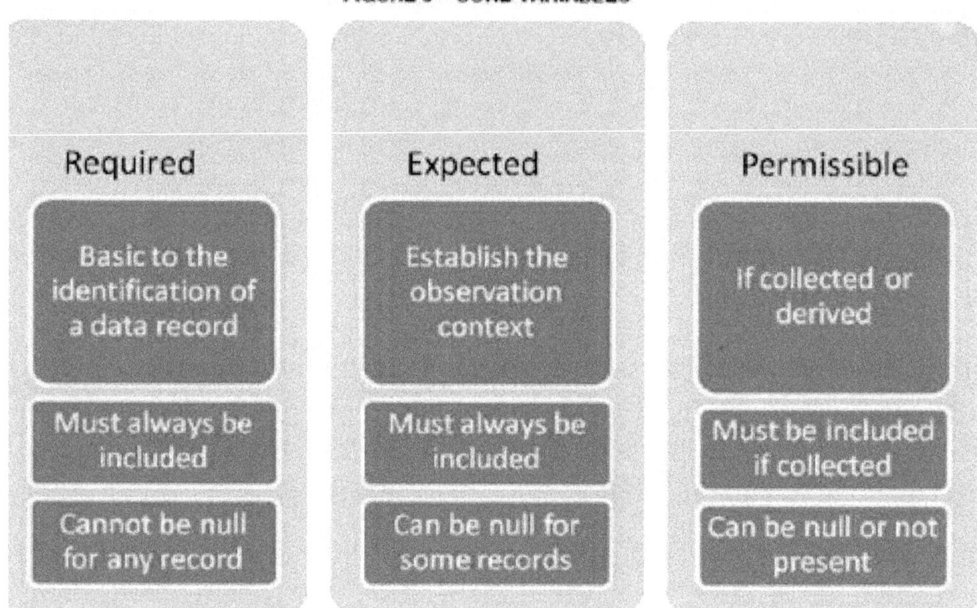

Messages to be checked in the LOG Window?

Messages to be Checked in the LOG Window in SAS:

1. **ERRORS**: Indicates critical issues encountered during program execution that prevent successful completion. These must be resolved to ensure accurate results.

2. **WARNINGS**: Alerts about potential issues that may affect the validity or reliability of results. While not critical, they warrant attention and may require adjustments to the program.

3. **NOTES**: Provides supplementary information about program execution, such as dataset creation, variable attributes, or options used. Useful for understanding program flow and ensuring correct implementation.

4. **SAS WENT TO A NEWLINE**: Indicates when SAS processing exceeds the current line length and continues on the next line. While not an error, it may affect code readability and should be monitored to avoid unintended line breaks.

1. **NUMERIC VALUES CONVERTED TO CHARACTER VALUES**: Indicates conversion of numeric data to character data, which may affect data integrity and analysis.

2. **CHARACTER VALUES CONVERTED TO NUMERIC VALUES**: Signifies conversion of character data to numeric data, potentially impacting data accuracy and analysis.

3. **VARIABLE UNINITIALIZED**: Alerts when a variable is not initialized with a value before being used, which may lead to unexpected results.

4. **DATASET WITH 0 OBSERVATIONS**: Indicates a dataset that was created but contains no observations, potentially due to data processing issues or filtering criteria.

5. **MERGE STATEMENT HAS MORE THAN ONE DATASET WITH REPEATED BY VARIABLES**: Warns when a MERGE statement includes multiple datasets with repeated BY variables, which may cause unexpected merging results.

6. **W.D FORMAT IS TOO SMALL TO PRINT**: Indicates that the width and decimal format specified for a variable is insufficient to display its value accurately, potentially leading to truncated output.

7. **UNBALANCED QUOTATION MARK**: Alerts when there is a mismatch in the number of opening and closing quotation marks in the code, which can cause syntax errors.

8. **REFERENCED VARIABLE NOT FOUND IN DATASET**: Indicates when a variable referenced in the program code is not present in the specified dataset, potentially due to misspellings or dataset changes.

9. **LENGTH HAS ALREADY BEEN SET/DEFINED**: Alerts when the length of a variable has been previously defined and attempted to redefine, which may cause conflicts or unexpected behavior.

10. **INVALID ARGUMENT TO FUNCTION**: Indicates when an incorrect argument is provided to a function or procedure, potentially leading to errors in program execution.

11. **STOPPED**: Indicates premature termination of the program execution, usually due to an error or interruption.

12. **REPLACED**: Signifies that a value or portion of code has been replaced during processing, often used in data manipulation or transformation.

13. **TRUNCATED**: Indicates that data or output has been truncated, typically due to limitations in storage or display capacity.

14. **UNKNOWN**: Indicates an unidentified or unrecognized message, which may require further investigation or clarification.

What is Mean Median STD Min Max?

Certainly! Here are the definitions and formulas for each statistical measure:
   1. **Mean**:
- Definition: The mean, often referred to as the average, is the sum of all values in a dataset divided by the total number of values.
2. **Median**:
- Definition: The median is the middle value in a dataset when the values are arranged in ascending or descending order. If there is an even number of observations, the median is the average of the two middle values.
3. **Standard Deviation**:
- Definition: The standard deviation measures the dispersion or variability of the values in a dataset. It indicates how much the values deviate from the mean.
- Formula:
$$\text{Standard Deviation} (s) = \sqrt{\frac{\sum_{i=1}^{n}(x_i - \bar{x})^2}{n-1}}$$
where x_i represents each individual value in the dataset, $\bar{x}$ is the mean, and n is the total number of values.
   4. **Minimum**:
- Definition: The minimum value in a dataset is the smallest value observed.
5. **Maximum**:
- Definition: The maximum value in a dataset is the largest value observed.
These measures provide insights into the central tendency, spread, and range of values in a dataset, aiding in data analysis and interpretation.

Distinction between 'Actual Treatment' and 'Planned Treatment

In clinical trials, "Actual Treatment" refers to the treatment or intervention that participants actually receive during the course of the study. This includes the specific medications, therapies, procedures, or other interventions administered to participants as per the study protocol.

On the other hand, "Planned Treatment" refers to the treatment or intervention that is specified in the study protocol prior to participant enrollment. It outlines the intended regimen or procedures that participants are supposed to receive during the study.

The comparison between actual and planned treatment is essential for assessing protocol adherence, evaluating the effectiveness of the intervention, and understanding any deviations from the intended treatment plan. It helps ensure the integrity and reliability of the study results.

DEFINE.XML

Define.xml serves multiple purposes throughout the data collection and reporting process in clinical trials:

- It provides specifications to data providers, facilitating accurate data collection and submission.
- Enables comparison of received data against specified requirements, ensuring data quality and compliance.
- Offers data description for internal users such as data reviewers and statisticians, aiding in data interpretation and analysis.
- Supports data archiving by serving as a comprehensive 'table of contents' for a company's data repository.

Creating Define.xml Files Using P-21:

1. **Prepare Standard Specification File**:
- Utilize XPT files to develop a standard specification file outlining domains, variables, and controlled terminology.

2. **Run and Update Specification Files**:
- Execute the main macro to generate Define.xml files based on the standard specification file.
- Update specification files with additional information and validate against datasets to ensure accuracy.

3. **Define.xml Creation Tab**:
- Use the Define.xml creation tab to create Define.xml files, incorporating metadata specifications and data validation results.

4. **Apply Macros for Hyperlink Each Term**:
- Apply macros to hyperlink each term in the Define.xml files, enhancing accessibility and navigation within the document.

By following these steps, organizations can effectively utilize P-21 to develop Define.xml files, ensuring comprehensive metadata standards and regulatory compliance in clinical trials.

DM (Demographics) - [SDTMIG 3.1.2]   Location: dm.xpt

Variable	Label / Description	Type	Length or Display Format	Controlled Terms or ISO Format	Origin / Source / Method / Comment
	Related Supplemental Qualifiers Dataset: SUPPDM (Supplemental Qualifiers for DM)				
STUDYID	Study Identifier	text	7		Protocol (Source: Sponsor)
DOMAIN	Domain Abbreviation	text	2	Domain Abbreviation (DM) • "DM" = "Demographics"	Assigned (Source: Sponsor)
USUBJID	Unique Subject Identifier	text	14		Derived (Source: Sponsor) Concatenation of STUDYID and SUBJID
SUBJID	Subject Identifier for the Study	text	6		Collected (Source: Investigator) Annotated CRF [3]
RFSTDTC	Subject Reference Start Date/Time	date		ISO 8601	Derived (Source: Sponsor) RFSTDTC = first date/time of study drug, for safety subject. Null for screen failures.

define.xml one page

Blinding & Unblinding

In clinical trials, blinding refers to the process of keeping certain information concealed from participants, researchers, or both, to minimize bias and ensure the integrity of the study results. Unblinding, on the other hand, is the intentional or unintentional revelation of this concealed information.

Here's a breakdown of both terms:

1. **Blinding**:

- **Single-Blind**: In a single-blind trial, either the participants or the researchers are unaware of which treatment is being administered. This prevents bias that could influence the outcomes.

- **Double-Blind**: In a double-blind trial, both the participants and the researchers are unaware of who is receiving the treatment and who is receiving a placebo or alternative treatment. This further reduces bias and enhances the reliability of the results.

- **Triple-Blind**: In some cases, a third party, such as the data analysts, may also be blinded to the treatment assignments. This is known as a triple-blind trial and adds an additional layer of impartiality to the study.

2. **Unblinding**:

- **Intentional Unblinding**: Occurs when the blinding is intentionally lifted during the study, often for ethical or safety reasons. This could happen if a participant experiences a severe adverse reaction, and knowing their treatment assignment becomes crucial for their medical care.

- **Unintentional Unblinding**: Can occur due to various factors such as accidental disclosure of treatment assignments, data entry errors, or unanticipated interactions between participants and researchers. Unintentional unblinding can introduce bias and compromise the validity of the study results.

Overall, blinding is a crucial methodological strategy in clinical trials to minimize bias and ensure the reliability of the study findings. Unblinding should be carefully managed and documented to maintain the integrity of the trial.

process in SAS programming:

1. **Dummy Dataset Creation**:

- Generate a dummy dataset containing participant information and dummy treatments, ensuring blinding of treatment assignments.

- Utilize pseudorandomization techniques to assign treatments while maintaining blinding throughout the study.

2. **Dynamic ARM and ARMCD Handling**:

- Implement dynamic handling of ARM and ARMCD variables to accommodate changes in treatment assignments during the study.

- Update ARM and ARMCD variables as per new treatments received by participants, ensuring accurate representation of treatment arms.

3. **Blinding Maintenance During Study**:

- Implement blinding mechanisms throughout the study duration to prevent unintentional unblinding of treatment assignments.

- Utilize coding conventions or masking techniques to conceal treatment information from participants and researchers.

4. **Transition to Actual Dataset**:

- Upon completion of the study, transition from the dummy dataset to the actual dataset provided by the sponsor.

- Ensure seamless integration of blinded data from the dummy dataset with unblinded data from the actual dataset.

    5. **Affecting Domains Handling**:

- Address changes in domains such as ADSL and DM EX due to the introduction of new treatments during the study.
- Update domain variables and metadata to reflect modifications in treatment assignments and ensure consistency across datasets.

By implementing these steps in SAS programming, researchers can effectively handle the blinding process in clinical trials, ensuring integrity and reliability of the study results despite changes in treatment assignments.

Types of Figure's you generated regulary

1. **Scatter Plots**: Visual representation of data points plotted on a two-dimensional graph, showing the relationship between two continuous variables. Useful for identifying patterns, trends, and correlations in the data.

2. **Line Plots or Series Plots**: Graphical representation of data points connected by straight lines, illustrating the trend or change in a variable over time or another continuous dimension.

3. **Box Plot (Whisker Plot)**: Graphical summary of a dataset's distribution, displaying the median, quartiles, and outliers. It provides insights into the central tendency and spread of the data.

4. **Odds Ratio Plot**: Visualization of odds ratios and confidence intervals for comparing the odds of an event between two or more groups. Useful for assessing the strength and direction of associations in categorical data.

5. **Kaplan-Meier Plot**: Graphical representation of survival data, showing the proportion of participants surviving over time in a clinical study. It is commonly used in time-to-event analysis, such as in survival analysis or clinical trials.

6. **Histograms**: Visual representation of the distribution of a continuous variable, depicting the frequency or count of observations falling within predefined intervals or bins.

7. **Bar Charts**: Graphical representation of categorical data using rectangular bars, with the height or length of each bar representing the frequency or count of observations in each category. Useful for comparing the distribution of categorical variables.

These figures are essential tools in exploratory data analysis, hypothesis testing, and result visualization in SAS. They help researchers and analysts gain insights into their data and communicate findings effectively.

Statistical Analysis Plan (SAP) outline

The Statistical Analysis Plan (SAP) outlines the methodology and procedures for conducting statistical analysis in a clinical trial. Contents typically include:

1. **Introduction**: Presents study objectives, design, and duration, as well as details on randomization.

2. **Elaboration of Study Protocol**: Discusses study populations, endpoints (including primary and secondary efficacy endpoints), and sample size determination.

3. **Statistical Methods**:
- General overview.
- Summary of study population information, including patient disposition, demographics, and study drug compliance.
- Analysis of study endpoints, such as primary efficacy, secondary efficacy, and safety analyses.
- Handling of missing data, protocol deviations, and key data items.
- Planned protocol analysis changes.

4. **Output Planned for the Study Report**:
- Tables to be included in the study report, covering subject disposition, baseline characteristics, efficacy, and safety results.
- Listings to be included, such as subject disposition, demographics, study drug accountability, and clinical data.
- Figures to be included in the study report.

5. **References**.

6. **Attachment**: Provides shells of tables, figures, and listings planned for the Clinical Study Report.

Overall, the SAP serves as a comprehensive guide for conducting statistical analysis in the clinical trial and ensures transparency and consistency in reporting results.

Why did you used data _null_?

Using `data _null_` allows us to generate customized reports directly from the data step without creating a dataset. This approach is beneficial when our goal is to produce a report rather than store data.

By leveraging `data _null_`, we can execute data manipulation and analysis steps while bypassing dataset creation, thus optimizing efficiency and conserving storage space.

How many tables/listings/figures and adam sdtm have you worked on day?

To provide an estimate, I typically work on:
- **Tables**: Approximately 4 hours for initial creation and 2 hours for replication.
- **Listings**: Around 2 hours for initial creation and 2 hours for replication.
- **Figures (ADaM)**: Typically 4-8 hours for complex figures and 2 hours for replication.
- **SDTM**: About 4 hours for initial creation and 2 hours for replication.

However, the actual time spent can vary based on the complexity of the work and project submission timelines. These estimates are provided as a general guideline and may be adjusted accordingly.

Did you generate Confidence Intervals? and procudres used

Confidence intervals are statistical ranges that estimate the likely range of values for a population parameter based on sample data, providing a measure of uncertainty around the estimate.

Here are some SAS procedures commonly used for generating confidence intervals:

1. **PROC MEANS**: Calculates summary statistics including means and can generate confidence intervals for means.

2. **PROC FREQ**: Computes frequencies and percentages for categorical variables and can also produce confidence intervals for proportions.

3. **PROC UNIVARIATE**: Computes descriptive statistics such as means, standard deviations, and percentiles, and can generate confidence intervals for these statistics.

4. **PROC GLM**: Performs analysis of variance (ANOVA) and regression analysis and can produce confidence intervals for model parameters.

5. **PROC TTEST**: Conducts t-tests for means of continuous variables and can output confidence intervals for differences in means.

6. **PROC SURVEYMEANS**: Computes summary statistics for survey data and can generate confidence intervals that account for complex survey designs.

These procedures offer various options and functionalities for calculating confidence intervals based on the specific needs of the analysis.

Types of ADaM datasets CDISC

ADaM datasets, according to CDISC standards, encompass various types designed to organize and analyze clinical trial data systematically. Some common ADaM datasets include:

ADaM Basic Data Structure (BDS): Contains trial data organized for statistical analysis, facilitating comprehensive analyses across different domains.

BDS (Basic Data Structure) datasets store key information about subjects and visits, often including:

SUBJECTID: Identifier for each subject.

VISIT: Visit identifier.

PARAMCD: Parameter code, similar to ADSL, providing standardized identification for the measured variable.

AVISIT: Actual visit time, specifying the date and time of the visit.

Analysis Datasets (ADSL): Focuses on analysis-ready datasets containing key variables for statistical analysis, including efficacy and safety assessments.

datasets typically contain one record per subject and are organized to facilitate analysis of longitudinal data

ADSL (Analysis Data Structure - Longitudinal) datasets typically include basic demographic and characteristic variables for each subject, providing essential information for longitudinal data analysis. These variables commonly include:

SUBJECTID: Identifier for each subject in the study.

AGE: Age of the subject at baseline or each visit.

SEX: Gender or sex of the subject.

RACE: Ethnic or racial background of the subject.

POPULATION: Population subgroup to which the subject belongs.

FALFS: A flag variable indicating if the subject has experienced a treatment failure or not.

Occurrence Data Structure (OCCDS): Specifically captures data related to adverse events, enabling thorough analysis and reporting of safety outcomes.

OCCDS (Occurrence Data Structure) datasets focus on capturing data related to adverse events, typically including:

STUDYID: Identifier for the study.

SUBJECTID: Identifier for each subject.

AESTDTC: Start date of the adverse event.

AEENDTC: End date of the adverse event.

AEDECOD: MedDRA code for the adverse event.

Non-standard ADaM datasets: Customized datasets tailored to specific study needs, which may include additional variables or modifications beyond standard CDISC specifications.

These ADaM datasets serve distinct purposes in clinical data analysis, ensuring consistency, efficiency, and compliance with regulatory requirements throughout the research process.

Tell me some ADaM and SDTM datasets you worked on?

1. **TA (Trial Arms)**:
- Type: Trial Design
- Description: One record per planned element per arm
2. **TE (Trial Elements)**:
- Type: Trial Design
- Description: One record per planned element
3. **TI (Trial Inclusion/Exclusion Criteria)**:
- Type: Trial Design
- Description: One record per inclusion/exclusion criterion
4. **TV (Trial Visits)**:
- Type: Trial Design
- Description: One record per planned visit per arm
5. **TS (Trial Summary)**:
- Type: Trial Design
- Description: One record per trial summary parameter value
6. **AE (Adverse Events)**:
- Type: Events
- Description: One record per adverse event per subject
7. **CM (Concomitant Medications)**:
- Type: Interventions
- Description: One record per recorded intervention occurrence or constant-dosing interval per subject
8. **DM (Demographics)**:
- Type: Special Purpose Domains
- Description: One record per subject
9. **DS (Disposition)**:
- Type: Events
- Description: One record per disposition status or protocol milestone per subject
10. **IE (Inclusion/Exclusion Criteria Not Met)**:
- Type: Findings
- Description: One record per inclusion/exclusion criterion not met per subject

ADaM Safety:
1. **ADSL (Subject Level Analysis Dataset)**:
- Type: Subject Level Analysis Dataset
- Description: One record per subject.
2. **ADAE (Adverse Event Analysis Dataset)**:
- Type: Occurrence Data Structure

- Description: One record per adverse event per subject.
   3. **ADCM (Concomitant Medications Analysis Dataset)**:
- Type: Occurrence Data Structure
- Description: One record per medication intervention per subject.
   4. **ADMH (Medical History Analysis Dataset)**:
- Type: Occurrence Data Structure
- Description: One record per medical history event per subject.
   5. **ADEX (Exposure Analysis Dataset)**:
- Type: Occurrence Data Structure
- Description: One record per constant dosing interval per subject.
   6. **ADPE (Physical Examinations Analysis Dataset)**:
- Type: Basic Data Structure
- Description: One record per parameter per time point per subject.
   7. **ADEG (ECG Test Results Analysis Dataset)**:
- Type: Basic Data Structure
- Description: One record per parameter per time point per subject.
   8. **ADFA (Findings About Analysis Dataset)**:
- Type: Basic Data Structure
- Description: One record per parameter per time point per subject.
   9. **ADLB (Laboratory Test Results Analysis Dataset)**:
- Type: Basic Data Structure
- Description: One record per parameter per time point per subject.
   10. **ADVS (Vital Signs Analysis Dataset)**:
- Type: Basic Data Structure
- Description: One record per parameter per time point per subject.

ADaM Efficacy:

Here's the information presented in a concise point-wise format:
   1. **ADTTE (ADaM dataset for Time to Opioid Uses - First and Last)**:
- Type: Basic Data Structure
- Description: Contains data related to the time to first and last opioid use for each subject.
- Structure: One record per parameter (time to first and last opioid use) per time point per subject.
   2. **ADQS (Questionnaires Analysis Dataset)**:
- Type: Basic Data Structure
- Description: Contains data from questionnaires administered during the study.
- Structure: One record per parameter per time point per subject.
   3. **ADMB (Microbiology Specimen Analysis Dataset)**:
- Type: Basic Data Structure
- Description: Contains data related to microbiology specimens collected during the study.
- Structure: One record per parameter per time point per subject.
   4. **ADRS (Response Analyses)**:
- Analyzes subjects' responses to treatment.
- One record per subject per analysis parameter.
   5. **ADTR (Tumor Results Analyses)**:
- Analyzes tumor-related results.
- One record per subject per analysis parameter per analysis date.

Mix keyword and positional parameters in Macros

In SAS macros, you can indeed mix keyword and positional parameters. This feature allows for more flexible and readable macro calls.

```
%macro example(param1, param2=10, param3);
/* Macro code */
%put Param1: &param1, Param2: &param2, Param3: &param3;
%mend;
    /* Macro call with positional parameters */
%example(value1, value3);
    /* Macro call with keyword parameters */
%example(param1=value1, param3=value3);
    /* Macro call with a mix of positional and keyword parameters */
%example(value1, param3=value3);
```

In the last macro call, `value1` is a positional parameter, and `value3` is a keyword parameter. Mixing them allows you to provide default values for some parameters while specifying others explicitly.

In Proc Report, if you want to sort by formatted value, how do you do that.

In SAS `PROC REPORT`, if you want to sort by a formatted value, you can use the `SORT` statement along with the `FMTSEARCH` option to ensure that the formatted values are considered for sorting.

```
    proc report data=mydata;
columns var1 var2;
define var1 / order;
define var2 / display;
/* Sorting by formatted value of var1 */
compute before _page_;
call define('_c1_', 'order', 'formatted');
endcomp;
run;
```

In this example:

- `var1` is the variable you want to sort by.
- `var2` is another variable you want to display in the report.
- `compute before _page_;` is used to control the sorting.
- `call define('_c1_', 'order', 'formatted');` specifies that sorting should be based on the formatted values of `var1`.

Ensure that you replace `mydata`, `var1`, and `var2` with your actual dataset name and variable names. Additionally, the `'formatted'` option in the `call define` statement tells SAS to consider the formatted values for sorting.

Have you used Proc SQL. When will you use 'Having' clause? What is meant by 'Outer Join'?

Yes, I'm familiar with `PROC SQL`. The `HAVING` clause in SQL is used with the `GROUP BY` clause to filter groups based on aggregate values. It is applied after the `GROUP BY` clause and before the `ORDER BY` clause.

You would use the `HAVING` clause when you want to filter the groups returned by a `GROUP BY` clause based on some condition involving aggregate functions such as `SUM`, `AVG`, `COUNT`, etc. For example:

SELECT department, AVG(salary) AS avg_salary
FROM employees
GROUP BY department
HAVING avg_salary > 50000;

This query selects the department and calculates the average salary for each department. Then, it filters out departments where the average salary is greater than $50,000 using the `HAVING` clause.

An 'Outer Join' is a type of join operation in SQL that returns all rows from one table (or both tables) even if there is no match in the other table. It's particularly useful when you want to include all records from one table, regardless of whether there's a corresponding match in the other table.

There are three types of outer joins:

1. **LEFT OUTER JOIN**: Returns all rows from the left table, and the matched rows from the right table. If there is no match, the result is NULL in the columns from the right table.

2. **RIGHT OUTER JOIN**: Returns all rows from the right table, and the matched rows from the left table. If there is no match, the result is NULL in the columns from the left table.

3. **FULL OUTER JOIN**: Returns all rows when there is a match in either the left or right table. If there is no match, the result is NULL in the columns from the table that lacks a matching row.

Outer joins are commonly used when you want to include unmatched rows from one table with matched rows from another table, or when you want to include all rows from both tables in the result set.

How can you create spread sheet from SAS?

You can create spreadsheets from SAS in several ways.

One common method is to use the `PROC EXPORT` procedure, which allows you to export SAS datasets into various file formats including Excel spreadsheets. Here's a basic example:

```
/* Exporting a SAS dataset to an Excel spreadsheet */
proc export data=mydataset
outfile='path\to\output\file.xlsx'
dbms=xlsx
replace;
run;
```

In this example:
- `mydataset` is the name of your SAS dataset.
- `'path\to\output\file.xlsx'` is the path where you want to save your Excel spreadsheet.
- `dbms=xlsx` specifies that you want to export the dataset to an Excel file.
- `replace` is an optional statement that replaces the existing file if it already exists.

You can also customize the export process by specifying options like `SHEET`, `DBLABEL`, `SHEET_INTERVAL`, etc., depending on your requirements.

Alternatively, if you need more control over the formatting of your Excel spreadsheet or want to generate complex reports, you can use the SAS/ACCESS Interface to PC Files or the SAS ODS Excel destination. These methods offer more advanced features for creating Excel files directly from SAS.

Diff b/w use of double quotes and single quotes in titles

In SAS, both double quotes (" ") and single quotes (' ') can be used to define titles, but they serve slightly different purposes:

   1. **Double Quotes (" "):**

- Double quotes are used when you want to include macro variable references, special characters, or escape sequences within your title.

- SAS will resolve macro variable references enclosed in double quotes and interpret special characters and escape sequences.

- Example:

title "Average Salary for &department";

   2. **Single Quotes (' '):**

- Single quotes are used when you want to treat the text literally, without resolving macro variable references or interpreting special characters.

- SAS does not resolve macro variable references or interpret special characters and escape sequences enclosed in single quotes.

- Example:

   title 'Average Salary for &department';

In both cases, `&department` would be replaced with the value of the macro variable `department` if it exists and is resolved.

   Using the appropriate type of quotes depends on whether you want SAS to resolve macro variable references and interpret special characters or treat the text literally.

self-check on table. how did you check it?

In clinical SAS reports or any SAS reports in general, you can perform self-checks on tables to ensure accuracy and reliability of the data presented. Here's how you might typically do it:

1. **Verify Data Sources**: Double-check that the data used in the table is sourced from the correct datasets and variables. Ensure that the data extraction and manipulation processes are accurately reflected in the table.

2. **Variable Calculations**: If the table includes calculations or derived variables, review the code or logic used to create them. Cross-reference these calculations with the source data to confirm accuracy.

3. **Comparison with Previous Reports**: If this is a recurring report, compare the current table with tables from previous reports. Ensure consistency in data presentation and any trends or changes observed over time.

4. **Verify Aggregations and Summary Statistics**: For summary tables presenting aggregated data or summary statistics, independently calculate these values using the raw data to confirm accuracy.

5. **Check Formatting**: Review the formatting of the table, including headers, footnotes, and data presentation. Ensure that all elements are appropriately labeled and formatted according to the reporting standards.

6. **Data Validation**: Perform data validation checks to identify any outliers or inconsistencies in the data. This may involve running frequency checks, range checks, or other data validation procedures.

7. **Peer Review**: If possible, have a colleague or peer review the table independently. A fresh pair of eyes may catch errors or inconsistencies that were overlooked during the initial review.

8. **Documentation**: Document the validation steps performed on the table, including any discrepancies found and resolutions applied. This documentation serves as an audit trail for future reference.

By following these steps, you can conduct a thorough self-check on tables in clinical SAS reports to ensure the accuracy and reliability of the presented data.

Difference between + operator and sum function

In SAS, the `+` operator and the `SUM` function serve different purposes:

1. **`+` Operator**:
- The `+` operator is used for performing arithmetic addition between numeric values.
- It's typically used within expressions or statements to add numeric values together.
- It's an infix operator, meaning it's placed between the values being added.
- Example:

```
data example;
total = var1 + var2;
run;
```

- In this example, `total` will contain the sum of `var1` and `var2`.

2. **`SUM` Function**:
- The `SUM` function is used to calculate the total sum of numeric values within a group.
- It's commonly used with the `BY` statement in data step or in PROC steps to calculate sums within groups defined by one or more variables.
- It can also be used in a DATA step to accumulate totals.
- Example:

```
proc means data=mydata;
by groupvar;
var numericvar;
output out=summaries sum=sum_numericvar;
run;
```

- In this example, `SUM(numericvar)` calculates the sum of the variable `numericvar` within each group defined by `groupvar`.

In summary, the `+` operator is used for simple addition between two numeric values, while the `SUM` function is used for calculating sums, often within groups of data.

Difference between IF and WHERE

In SAS, both the `IF` and `WHERE` statements are used for data filtering, but they operate in different contexts and have different functionalities:

    1. **IF Statement**:

- The `IF` statement is primarily used within DATA step programming to conditionally execute statements based on logical conditions.
- It is used to subset observations within the data step based on specified conditions.
- It evaluates each observation individually and determines whether to execute the subsequent statements based on the condition specified.
- Example:

```
data newdata;
set olddata;
if condition then output;
run;
```

- In this example, only observations for which the condition is true are written to the output dataset `newdata`.

    2. **WHERE Statement**:

- The `WHERE` statement is used in DATA steps, PROC steps, and SQL queries to filter observations from a dataset or a result set based on specified conditions.
- It is used to subset observations before processing, rather than conditionally executing statements like the `IF` statement.
- It can be used to filter observations based on logical conditions, character or numeric comparisons, and combinations of conditions.
- Example (in PROC SQL):

```
proc sql;
select *
from mydata
where condition;
quit;
```

- In this example, only observations meeting the specified condition are selected from the dataset `mydata`.

In summary, the `IF` statement is used for conditional execution of statements within a DATA step, while the `WHERE` statement is used to filter observations from datasets or result sets based on specified conditions in DATA steps, PROC steps, and SQL queries.

What will happen to merging if there is difference in length

When merging datasets in SAS using a `MERGE` statement or a `JOIN` operation in PROC SQL, differences in variable lengths between the datasets being merged can lead to unexpected results. Here's what typically happens:

   1. **Mismatched Lengths**:
- If there is a difference in lengths between variables being merged, SAS will perform the merge based on the common length of the variables.
- For example, if you are merging a dataset where a variable is defined as length 8 and another dataset where the same variable is defined as length 12, SAS will consider the variable as length 8 during the merge.

   2. **Truncation**:
- If the variable lengths are different and the variable being merged from one dataset is longer than the same variable in the other dataset, truncation may occur.
- SAS will truncate the longer variable to match the length of the shorter variable during the merge.
- This can lead to loss of data or unexpected results if important information is truncated.

   3. **Warning Messages**:
- SAS may issue warning messages in the log to alert you to potential data loss due to truncation.
- These warning messages can help you identify situations where variable lengths are not aligned and could lead to unexpected results.

   To avoid issues related to differences in variable lengths during merging, it's essential to ensure consistency in variable lengths between datasets being merged. This can be achieved by:
- Standardizing variable lengths across datasets before merging.
- Using appropriate length specifications when creating or modifying variables.
- Reviewing log messages for any warnings related to variable truncation during merges.

Besides PROC Transpose any other way to transpose data

Yes, besides using PROC TRANSPOSE, there are alternative methods to transpose data in SAS. Here are a few common approaches:

1. **Data Step with Arrays:**

- You can use a DATA step with arrays to transpose data.
- This method involves reading the data row by row and then writing it out column by column.
- It requires creating a new dataset with the transposed structure.
- Example:

```
data transposed_data;
set original_data;
array var{10} var1-var10;
do i = 1 to dim(var);
transposed_var = var{i};
output;
end;
run;
```

2. **SQL with Case Statements**:

- You can use SQL queries with CASE statements to pivot the data.
- This method involves creating a new dataset with the transposed structure using conditional logic in SQL.
- Example:

```
proc sql;
create table transposed_data as
select
ID,
case when variable = 'var1' then value1
when variable = 'var2' then value2
...
else . end as transposed_var
from original_data;
quit;
```

3. **Hash Objects**:

- You can use hash objects to transpose data efficiently, especially for large datasets.
- This method involves loading the data into a hash object and then using the object to transpose the data.
- Example:

```
data transposed_data;
if _n_ = 1 then do;
declare hash h();
h.defineKey('variable');
h.defineData('value');
h.defineDone();
end;
set original_data;
h.replace();
do until(last.variable);
set original_data;
by variable;
transposed_var = value;
output;
end;
run;
```

These methods provide alternatives to PROC TRANSPOSE for transposing data in SAS, each with its advantages and suitability depending on the specific requirements of your data and analysis.

Creation ADaM specifications

Creating ADaM specifications involves several steps to ensure compliance with CDISC standards and to meet the requirements of the statistical analysis plan. Here's a general approach:

1. **Review CDISC Standards and Implementation Guide**:
- Familiarize yourself with CDISC ADaM standards and guidelines outlined in the Implementation Guide.
- Understand the structure and content requirements for ADaM datasets.

2. **Identify Outputs**:
- Review the statistical analysis plan to identify all required outputs, including table listings and figures.
- Determine the number of outputs needed and the variables required for each output.

3. **Define Variables**:
- Identify the variables needed to populate the required outputs.
- Include mandatory variables specified by CDISC standards for the respective dataset (e.g., ADaM datasets such as ADSL, ADLB, etc.).
- Derive additional variables as necessary to meet the requirements of the outputs and statistical analysis plan.
- Document variable derivations, including the logic and calculations used, referencing the statistical analysis plan where applicable.
- Collaborate with statisticians to clarify any uncertainties or to discuss theoretical derivations.

4. **Document Specifications**:
- Create ADaM specifications documents detailing the variables, derivations, and output requirements for each dataset.
- Organize the specifications logically, including sections for dataset structure, variable definitions, variable derivations, and output requirements.
- Ensure that the specifications document adheres to the format and guidelines specified in the CDISC Implementation Guide.
- Validate the specifications internally, ensuring consistency and accuracy of information.

5. **Review and Validation**:
- Submit the ADaM specifications for review by senior programmers and statisticians.
- Validate the specifications against the statistical analysis plan and CDISC standards to ensure completeness and accuracy.
- Incorporate feedback and revisions as necessary based on the review process.

6. **Programming Logic Implementation**:
- Once the ADaM specifications are finalized and validated, programmers can begin implementing the programming logic to derive the datasets.
- Follow the specifications document closely during programming to ensure consistency with the defined requirements.
- Document programming logic and code comments to provide transparency and facilitate future maintenance.

7. **Quality Control and Documentation**:
- Conduct quality control checks on the derived datasets to ensure accuracy and consistency with the specifications.
- Document any deviations from the specifications and the rationale behind them.

- Maintain clear and comprehensive documentation throughout the process to facilitate regulatory submissions and future reference.

By following these steps, you can create ADaM specifications that meet CDISC standards and accurately reflect the requirements of the statistical analysis plan. Collaboration with statisticians and senior programmers is essential to ensure the integrity and validity of the specifications.

Difference between RFXSTDTC and RFSTDTC

1. **RFXSTDTC (Earliest date of Protocol-specified treatment)**:
- This variable represents the earliest date when the protocol-specified treatment was administered to the subject.
- It indicates the start date of the treatment regimen specified in the study protocol.

2. **RFSTDTC (Treatment start date decided by Sponsor)**:
- This variable represents the treatment start date decided by the sponsor of the clinical trial.
- It may or may not coincide with the protocol-specified treatment start date (RFXSTDTC), depending on the specific study design and decisions made by the sponsor.

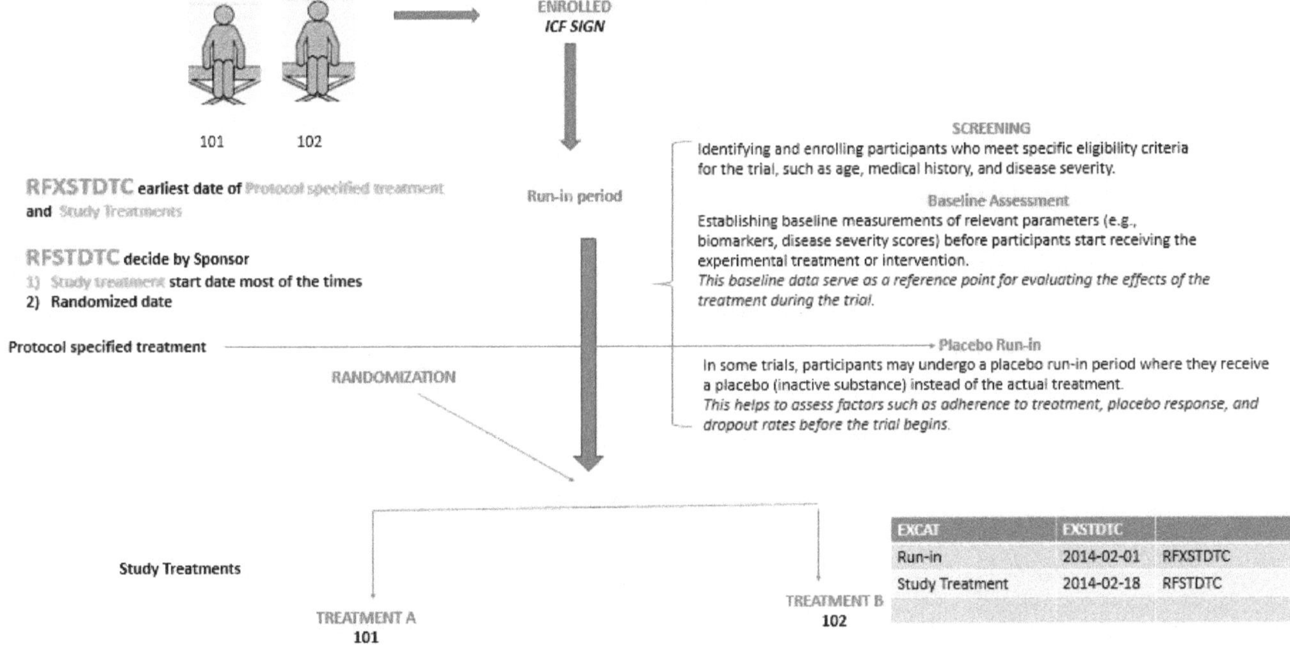

EXCAT	EXSTDTC	
Run-in	2014-02-01	RFXSTDTC
Study Treatment	2014-02-18	RFSTDTC

EC vs. EX SDTM Domains

In the SDTMIG, the Exposure (EX) domain is used to represent exposure to study treatment as described in the protocol.

The EC domain is used to represent data as collected on the CRF, and is used in a study when the SDTMIG EX domain cannot be directly populated with the data collected on the CRF.

Let's illustrate the difference between the Exposure (EX) and Events (EC) domains with a hypothetical example:

Suppose we are conducting a clinical trial to evaluate the efficacy and safety of a new medication for treating hypertension. In this trial, subjects are randomized to receive either the new medication or a placebo, and they are followed up over a period of 12 weeks.

1. **Exposure (EX) Domain**:
- In the EX domain, we would capture data related to the exposure of subjects to the study treatment as specified in the protocol.
- Variables in the EX domain might include:
- STUDYID: Study Identifier
- USUBJID: Unique Subject Identifier
- TRTSDTC: Treatment Start Date
- TRTEDTC: Treatment End Date
- ARMCD: Treatment Arm Code (e.g., active treatment or placebo)
- DOSE: Dose of Study Medication
- ROUTE: Route of Administration (e.g., oral, intravenous)
- Example record in the EX domain:

```
STUDYID | USUBJID | TRTSDTC | TRTEDTC | ARMCD | DOSE | ROUTE
------------------------------------------------------------------------
STUDY001 | 001-001 | 2024-01-01| 2024-03-31| Active | 100 mg | Oral
```

2. **Events (EC) Domain**:
- In the EC domain, we would capture data collected on the Case Report Form (CRF), which may include a wide range of events and information beyond treatment exposure.
- Variables in the EC domain might include:
- STUDYID: Study Identifier
- USUBJID: Unique Subject Identifier
- VISIT: Visit Name (e.g., Baseline, Week 4, Week 12)
- AESEV: Adverse Event Severity
- AETERM: Adverse Event Term
- CMTRT: Concomitant Medication Received
- MHSTDTC: Medical History Start Date
- MHENDTC: Medical History End Date
- Example record in the EC domain:

```
STUDYID | USUBJID | VISIT | AESEV | AETERM | CMTRT | MHSTDTC | MHENDTC
-------------------------------------------------------------------------------
STUDY001 | 001-001 | Baseline | Mild | Headache | None | |
STUDY001 | 001-001 | Week 4 | Severe | Hypotension | Amlodipine | |
STUDY001 | 001-001 | Week 12 | | | None | 2019-01-01| 2023-12-31
```

In this example, the EX domain captures data specifically related to the exposure of subjects to the study treatment, such as treatment start and end dates, dose, and route of administration. On the other hand, the EC domain captures a broader range of events and data collected during the study, including adverse events, concomitant medications, and medical history.

AE vs CE

Adverse Events (AEs) are indeed specific to untoward or undesirable medical occurrences.

Clinical Events (CEs) are broader, encompassing any significant **medical event of interest**, whether positive or negative, that may not necessarily meet the criteria of an adverse event.

Distinguish between Adverse Events (AEs) and Clinical Events (CEs):

1. **Adverse Events (AEs)**:
- Adverse Events are specific to untoward or undesirable medical occurrences experienced by subjects during the clinical trial.
- These events are typically adverse reactions to the study treatment or other interventions.
- AEs are usually assessed for severity and relationship to the study treatment.
- Examples of AEs include nausea, headache, hypotension, etc.

2. **Clinical Events (CEs)**:
- Clinical Events are broader and encompass any significant medical event of interest, whether positive or negative.
- CEs may include both favorable outcomes, such as successful treatment responses, as well as adverse events.
- They are not limited to adverse reactions but can also include positive outcomes or significant medical occurrences that are of interest in the study.
- Examples of CEs include successful treatment response, disease progression, hospitalization, etc.

Let's update the example to include both Adverse Events (AEs) and Clinical Events (CEs):

Adverse Events (AEs) Domain:
- Variables might include:
- STUDYID: Study Identifier
- USUBJID: Unique Subject Identifier
- AESEQ: Adverse Event Sequence Number
- AESER: Adverse Event Severity
- AETERM: Adverse Event Term
- AEACN: Adverse Event Action Taken
- Example record in the AEs domain:

```
STUDYID | USUBJID | AESEQ | AESER | AETERM | AEACN
-------------------------------------------------------------------
STUDY001 | 001-001 | 1 | Mild | Headache | Continue
STUDY001 | 001-001 | 2 | Severe| Hypotension | Stop
```

Clinical Events (CEs) Domain:
- Variables might include:
- STUDYID: Study Identifier
- USUBJID: Unique Subject Identifier
- CESEQ: Clinical Event Sequence Number
- CEDESC: Clinical Event Description
- Example record in the CEs domain:

```
STUDYID | USUBJID | CESEQ | CEDESC
--------------------------------------------
STUDY001 | 001-001 | 1 | Successful treatment response
STUDY001 | 001-001 | 2 | Hospitalization due to hypotension
```

In this refined example, the Adverse Events (AEs) domain captures specific adverse reactions experienced by subjects, while the Clinical Events (CEs) domain captures a broader range of significant medical events of interest, including both positive and negative outcomes.

What is ECMODE - Scheduled and performed

In the context of clinical trials and CDISC standards, ECMODE refers to the Mode of Collection for Events data. Specifically, ECMODE indicates how the data related to clinical events (such as adverse events or other significant medical occurrences) were scheduled and collected.

The values for ECMODE typically include:

1. **Scheduled**:

- Indicates that the collection of events data was planned and scheduled in advance according to the study protocol or data collection plan.
- Events were expected to be reported at specified time points or intervals during the course of the study.
- Data collection for events occurred according to a predetermined schedule.

2. **Performed**:

- Indicates that the collection of events data was actively performed or conducted during the study.
- Events were actively monitored, recorded, or reported as they occurred, rather than being collected according to a predefined schedule.
- Data collection for events was driven by actual occurrences or occurrences reported by subjects or healthcare providers during the study.

In summary, ECMODE - Scheduled indicates that events data collection was planned and scheduled according to the study protocol, while ECMODE - Performed indicates that events data collection was actively conducted or performed as events occurred during the study. These distinctions are important for understanding how events data were collected and reported in the clinical trial.

How do you Blank dataset in submission

In FDA submissions, when you need to submit a dataset that contains no data (i.e., a blank dataset), you typically follow specific guidelines to ensure compliance with regulatory requirements and to facilitate the review process. Here's how you can handle blank datasets in FDA submissions:

1. **Document the Intention**:
- Clearly document the intention to submit a blank dataset in your submission documentation, such as the Data Definition Document (DDD) or the Data Reviewer's Guide (DRG).
- Provide a rationale for why the dataset is blank and explain any implications for the study analysis or regulatory review.

2. **Include the Dataset Definition**:
- Include the dataset definition (metadata) for the blank dataset in the appropriate Define-XML (DEFINE) file.
- Define all variables and their attributes according to the Study Data Tabulation Model (SDTM) or Analysis Data Model (ADaM) standards.
- Ensure that variable names, lengths, formats, and labels are consistent with the data collection plan and the study protocol.

3. **Submit an Empty Dataset**:
- Create an empty dataset file (e.g., in SAS XPT format for SDTM datasets) containing only the dataset header and variable definitions.
- Populate the dataset file with appropriate metadata, including dataset name, dataset type (e.g., "LB" for laboratory data), and variable definitions.
- Ensure that the dataset file complies with regulatory requirements and follows the FDA's Electronic Common Technical Document (eCTD) format for electronic submissions.

4. **Provide Documentation and Justification**:
- Clearly document the reason for submitting a blank dataset and provide any necessary justifications in the submission package.
- Explain any circumstances or protocol deviations that led to the absence of data for the specified dataset.
- Include any relevant supporting documentation or correspondence with regulatory authorities regarding the blank dataset submission.

5. **Consult with Regulatory Authorities (if necessary)**:
- If you have concerns or uncertainties about submitting a blank dataset, consider consulting with regulatory authorities or seeking guidance from regulatory experts.
- Discuss the specific requirements and expectations for handling blank datasets in your submission.

By following these steps, you can appropriately handle blank datasets in FDA submissions, ensuring compliance with regulatory standards and facilitating the review process by regulatory authorities.

Not submitted variables – Any idea?

"Variables not submitted" refers to those variables that were planned to be collected or captured during the study but, for various reasons, were not included in the final dataset submitted for regulatory review. Here's how you can handle such variables in SDTM datasets:

1. **Documentation**:
- Document all variables that were originally planned to be collected but were not included in the final dataset.
- Provide a clear explanation for why these variables were not submitted. Common reasons include protocol amendments, changes in data collection procedures, data quality issues, or variables being deemed non-essential for regulatory review.

2. **Define-XML (DEFINE)**:
- Include metadata for variables not submitted in the Define-XML (DEFINE) file associated with the SDTM dataset.
- Define all variables, whether submitted or not, to maintain consistency in metadata documentation.

3. **Variable Status**:
- Use the appropriate variable status codes to indicate the status of variables not submitted.
- In SDTM, variables can have different statuses such as "Mandatory," "Expected," "Permissible," or "Not Collected." Variables not submitted would typically be assigned a status indicating that they were "Not Collected" or "Not Submitted."

4. **Justification**:
- Provide a clear justification for why each variable was not submitted.
- Include details on any protocol amendments, deviations, or other factors that influenced the decision not to include these variables in the final dataset.

5. **Reviewer's Guide**:
- Include information about variables not submitted in the Reviewer's Guide or other submission documentation.
- Explain the impact, if any, of these variables not being included on the interpretation of study results or the understanding of the study data.

6. **Regulatory Communication**:
- If necessary, communicate with regulatory authorities to discuss and justify the exclusion of certain variables from the submitted dataset.
- Provide any additional documentation or clarification requested by regulatory reviewers regarding variables not submitted.

By appropriately documenting and justifying variables not submitted in SDTM datasets, you can ensure transparency and regulatory compliance in the submission process.

Parallel and crossover studies

Parallel and crossover studies are two common designs used in clinical trials, each with distinct characteristics and purposes. Here's a brief overview of the differences between them:

    1. **Parallel Study**:

- In a parallel study design, participants are randomized into different treatment groups, and each group receives a different treatment regimen.
- Participants remain in their assigned treatment group for the duration of the study.
- Data from different treatment groups are compared at the end of the study to assess the efficacy and safety of the treatments.
- Parallel studies are suitable for comparing the effects of different treatments or interventions over a specified period.

    2. **Crossover Study**:

- In a crossover study design, participants receive multiple treatments or interventions in sequence, with each participant acting as their control.
- Participants may initially receive one treatment (the experimental treatment), followed by a washout period, and then receive another treatment (the control treatment).
- The order in which participants receive treatments is randomized to minimize bias.
- Each participant serves as their control, which helps reduce inter-subject variability and increases the study's statistical power.
- Crossover studies are often used to compare treatments within the same group of participants, allowing for a more efficient use of resources and reducing the required sample size.

    Key differences between parallel and crossover studies include:

    - **Design**: Parallel studies involve separate treatment groups receiving different interventions simultaneously, while crossover studies involve the same group of participants receiving multiple interventions in sequence.

    - **Duration**: Parallel studies typically have a fixed duration, with participants remaining in their assigned treatment groups for the entire study period. In contrast, crossover studies may have multiple treatment periods separated by washout periods, with participants receiving each treatment sequentially.

    - **Control**: In parallel studies, control groups may be included to provide a baseline for comparison with the treatment groups. In crossover studies, each participant serves as their control, reducing inter-subject variability.

    - **Analysis**: Data analysis in parallel studies involves comparing outcomes between different treatment groups. In crossover studies, analyses may include within-subject comparisons to assess the effects of different treatments within the same individuals.

    Both study designs have their advantages and limitations, and the choice between them depends on various factors, including the research question, the nature of the interventions, and practical considerations such as feasibility and ethical concerns.

Pinnacle21 warnings

1. NULL value in AEDECOD variable marked as Required
2. Missing End Time-Point value
3. Permissible variable with missing value for all records
4. No Details info for AESMIE Adverse Event in SUPPAE domain
5. Missing values for one or more variables subject to MedDRA: AELLT, AELLTCD, AEDECOD, AEPTCD, AEHLT, AEHLTCD, AEHLGT, AEHLGTCD, AEBODSYS, AEBDSYCD, AESOC, AESOCCD
6. CMDOSFRM value not found in 'Pharmaceutical Dosage Form' extensible codelist
7. CMDOSFRQ value not found in 'Frequency' extensible codelist
8. CMDOSU value not found in 'Unit' extensible codelist
9. CMROUTE value not found in 'Route of Administration Response' extensible codelist
10. NULL value in CMTRT variable marked as Required
11. Missing End Time-Point value
12. Missing Start Time-Point value
13. Missing values for CMSTDTC, CMSTRF and CMSTRTPT, when CMENDTC, CMENRF or CMENRTPT is provided
14. Value for CMENRF is populated, when RFENDTC is NULL
15. Permissible variable with missing value for all records
16. RACE value not found in 'Race' extensible codelist
17. NULL value in SEX variable marked as Required
18. Invalid ISO 8601 value for BRTHDTC variable
19. No baseline flag record in EG for subject
20. RFENDTC is not provided for a randomized subject
21. Unexpected character value in BRTHDTC variable
22. AGE is not provided

SDTM SRCVAR SRCDOM and SRCSEQ

In SDTM (Study Data Tabulation Model), SRCVAR, SRCDOM, and SRCSEQ are variables used to capture information related to the source of data or the origin of specific data points within a clinical trial. Here's what each of these variables typically represents:

1. **SRCVAR (Source Variable)**:
- SRCVAR is a variable that identifies the source data variable from which the SDTM variable is derived.
- It indicates the variable name or code used in the source system or original data collection instrument.
- SRCVAR helps establish traceability and transparency by linking SDTM variables to their corresponding source data variables.
- Example: SRCVAR="LAB01" may indicate that the SDTM laboratory test result variable (LBTEST) is derived from the source variable "LAB01" in the original data.

2. **SRCDOM (Source Domain)**:
- SRCDOM is a variable that identifies the source data domain or dataset from which the SDTM variable is derived.
- It indicates the source dataset or domain where the data originated before being mapped to SDTM format.
- SRCDOM provides context for understanding the origin of the data and facilitates cross-referencing between SDTM datasets and their source data.
- Example: SRCDOM="LB" may indicate that the SDTM laboratory test result variable (LBTEST) is derived from data in the laboratory dataset.

3. **SRCSEQ (Source Sequence Number)**:
- SRCSEQ is a variable that assigns a sequence number to individual data points or records within the source dataset.
- It helps establish the order or sequence of data collection within the source dataset.
- SRCSEQ provides additional granularity for traceability and allows for the identification of specific data points within the source data.
- Example: SRCSEQ=001 may indicate that the data point is the first record within the source dataset.

These variables play a crucial role in SDTM datasets by providing metadata that enables traceability, reproducibility, and transparency in clinical trial data analysis and interpretation. They help ensure that SDTM datasets accurately reflect the source data and facilitate the validation and quality assurance processes during the creation and review of clinical trial data.

Tracing of tumor information for hematology

In hematology oncology studies, tracing tumor information involves capturing and tracking data related to tumors and hematologic malignancies throughout the clinical trial process. Here's how tumor information can be traced:

1. **Identification of Tumor Types**:
- Define and document the specific types of tumors and hematologic malignancies being studied, including their histology, classification, and relevant diagnostic criteria.

2. **Tumor Identification at Baseline**:
- Capture baseline tumor information for each subject, including tumor type, size, location, stage, and any relevant biomarkers or genetic mutations.
- Use standardized assessment tools and imaging techniques (such as CT scans, MRI, PET scans, and bone marrow biopsies) to accurately characterize tumors at baseline.

3. **Tracking Tumor Progression and Response**:
- Regularly monitor and assess tumor response and progression during the course of the study, using standardized criteria such as RECIST (Response Evaluation Criteria in Solid Tumors) or Lugano criteria for lymphoma.
- Capture data on tumor size, volume, and metabolic activity, as well as any changes in tumor burden or disease status over time.

4. **Assessment of Hematologic Parameters**:
- In addition to tumor-specific assessments, track hematologic parameters such as complete blood counts (CBC), differential counts, hemoglobin levels, platelet counts, and coagulation profiles.
- Monitor changes in hematologic parameters over time, including any abnormalities or deviations from baseline values that may indicate disease progression or treatment-related toxicity.

5. **Documentation and Reporting**:
- Document all tumor-related data in a standardized format, such as the SDTM (Study Data Tabulation Model), to ensure consistency and interoperability across datasets.
- Include detailed annotations and descriptions of tumor assessments, response criteria used, and any deviations from protocol-specified procedures.
- Generate regular reports and summaries of tumor response, progression, and other relevant endpoints for review by investigators, regulatory authorities, and other stakeholders.

6. **Quality Control and Assurance**:
- Implement quality control measures to ensure the accuracy, completeness, and reliability of tumor data throughout the study.
- Conduct regular data review and validation checks to identify and resolve any discrepancies or inconsistencies in tumor information.

By carefully tracing tumor information in hematology oncology studies, researchers can gain valuable insights into disease progression, treatment efficacy, and patient outcomes, ultimately contributing to the development of new therapies and improvements in patient care.

Psoriasis, severity measured? how was score derived (Dermatology)

In dermatology, particularly in the context of psoriasis, the severity of the condition is commonly measured using standardized assessment tools and scoring systems. One of the most widely used scoring systems for assessing psoriasis severity is the Psoriasis Area and Severity Index (PASI). Here's how the PASI score is derived:

1. **Background**:
- The PASI is a clinical tool used to quantify the severity of psoriasis based on the extent of involvement (area) and the degree of erythema (redness), induration (thickness), and scaling (desquamation) of psoriatic lesions.

2. **Anatomic Regions**:
- The body is divided into four main anatomic regions: the head (H), trunk (T), upper extremities (UE), and lower extremities (LE).
- Each region is scored separately based on the extent and severity of psoriatic involvement.

3. **Lesion Assessment**:
- Within each anatomic region, psoriatic lesions are assessed and scored based on three main parameters: erythema, induration, and scaling.
- Each parameter is assigned a score ranging from 0 to 4, with 0 indicating no involvement and 4 indicating severe involvement.

4. **Scoring Calculation**:
- The PASI score for each region is calculated by summing the scores for erythema, induration, and scaling and multiplying by a weighting factor corresponding to the area of involvement.
- The PASI score for the entire body is then calculated by summing the scores for all four anatomic regions.

5. **Total PASI Score**:
- The total PASI score ranges from 0 to 72, with higher scores indicating greater disease severity.
- PASI scores can be categorized into different severity levels, such as mild, moderate, severe, and very severe, based on predefined cutoff values.

6. **Interpretation**:
- The PASI score provides an objective measure of psoriasis severity and is used to assess treatment response, monitor disease progression, and guide treatment decisions in clinical practice and research settings.

Other scoring systems and assessment tools may also be used to evaluate psoriasis severity, depending on the specific study or clinical context. However, the PASI score is widely recognized and commonly employed due to its reliability, reproducibility, and sensitivity to changes in disease severity.

Neuroscience (Alzheimer's) – primary endpoint, Quality of life

In neuroscience, particularly in Alzheimer's disease research, primary endpoints and quality of life assessments play crucial roles in evaluating the efficacy and impact of interventions. Here's how these concepts are relevant:

1. **Primary Endpoint**:
- The primary endpoint in Alzheimer's disease clinical trials typically refers to the main outcome measure used to assess the treatment's effectiveness or efficacy.
- Common primary endpoints in Alzheimer's trials include measures of cognitive function, such as changes in scores on standardized neuropsychological tests like the Mini-Mental State Examination (MMSE) or the Alzheimer's Disease Assessment Scale-Cognitive Subscale (ADAS-Cog).
- Other primary endpoints may include measures of functional ability, such as activities of daily living (ADL) or instrumental activities of daily living (IADL), which assess a person's ability to perform everyday tasks independently.
- The selection of a primary endpoint is critical for determining the success or failure of a clinical trial and often reflects the primary treatment target or mechanism of action.

2. **Quality of Life Assessment**:
- Quality of life (QoL) assessments in Alzheimer's disease research focus on evaluating the impact of the disease and interventions on patients' overall well-being, functioning, and subjective experience.
- QoL assessments may include self-reported measures, caregiver-reported measures, or observer-rated assessments that capture various domains of life quality, such as physical health, psychological well-being, social relationships, and environmental factors.
- Commonly used QoL instruments in Alzheimer's research include the Quality of Life-Alzheimer's Disease (QoL-AD) scale, the Alzheimer's Disease Related Quality of Life (ADRQL) scale, and generic QoL measures like the EuroQol Five-Dimension (EQ-5D) questionnaire.
- QoL assessments provide valuable insights into the broader impact of Alzheimer's disease on patients and caregivers and can inform treatment decisions and healthcare interventions aimed at improving overall well-being and functioning.

In summary, primary endpoints and quality of life assessments are essential components of clinical trials and research in Alzheimer's disease neuroscience. While primary endpoints focus on objective measures of treatment efficacy, QoL assessments provide valuable insights into the subjective experience and broader impact of the disease on individuals' lives, helping to guide holistic patient-centered care and intervention strategies.

Did you use Proc report. ID option

the ID option in PROC REPORT is commonly used to ensure that information about the same variable **continues on subsequent pages when the report spans multiple pages.**

When you want to display the same variable information on the next page, you typically include that variable in the ID statement. Here's how you might do it

```
proc report data=mydata nowd;
column IDVar1 IDVar2 Var1 Var2;
define IDVar1 / group id;
define IDVar2 / group;
define Var1 / analysis mean;
define Var2 / analysis sum;
define Var1 / display; /* Display Var1 again on the next page */
define Var2 / display; /* Display Var2 again on the next page */
run;
```

The nowd option in the PROC REPORT statement ensures that the report is not wrapped, meaning each page will display a fixed set of data.

IDVar1 is defined as a group variable with the id option to display its values.

IDVar2 is defined as a group variable.

Var1 and Var2 are defined as analysis variables.

Var1 and Var2 are also defined with the display option, which ensures that their values will be displayed again on the next page if the report spans multiple pages.

Extract Last Three Characters from Character Variable

To extract the last three characters from a character variable in SAS, you can use the SUBSTR function along with the LENGTH function to determine the length of the variable. Here's how you can do it:

data output;
set input;
last_three = substr(variable, length(variable) - 2);
run;

In this code:
- `input` is the input dataset containing the character variable you want to extract the last three characters from.
- `variable` is the name of the character variable from which you want to extract the last three characters.
- `last_three` is the new variable where the last three characters will be stored.
- The SUBSTR function is used to extract a substring from the `variable` starting from the position determined by `length(variable) - 2`, which represents the third character from the end of the string to the end of the string.
- This code assumes that the length of the `variable` is at least three characters long. If it's shorter, you may need to add additional logic to handle such cases.

ISS ISE

In clinical trials, ISS (Integrated Summary of Safety) and ISE (Integrated Summary of Efficacy) are comprehensive documents that provide a consolidated analysis of safety and efficacy data, respectively, from all relevant studies conducted as part of a drug development program. Here's a brief overview of ISS and ISE studies:

1. **Integrated Summary of Safety (ISS)**:
- The ISS is a regulatory document that presents an integrated analysis of safety data from multiple studies conducted during the clinical development of a drug.
- It includes data from all phases of clinical trials (Phase I, II, and III) as well as post-marketing studies.
- The ISS synthesizes safety information across different patient populations, dosages, and treatment durations to provide a comprehensive understanding of the safety profile of the investigational drug.
- Key components of the ISS may include summaries of adverse events, laboratory abnormalities, vital signs, and other safety parameters.

2. **Integrated Summary of Efficacy (ISE)**:
- The ISE is a regulatory document that provides an integrated analysis of efficacy data from all relevant studies conducted during the drug development process.
- Similar to the ISS, the ISE incorporates data from all phases of clinical trials and post-marketing studies to assess the effectiveness of the investigational drug.
- The ISE evaluates efficacy endpoints, such as primary and secondary endpoints defined in the study protocols, and may include analyses of efficacy across different patient subgroups and treatment regimens.
- The ISE aims to provide a comprehensive overview of the therapeutic effects of the investigational drug based on the available clinical evidence.

Both the ISS and ISE play critical roles in the regulatory submission process for drug approval. These documents are typically included in the Marketing Authorization Application (MAA) or New Drug Application (NDA) submitted to regulatory agencies such as the FDA (Food and Drug Administration) in the United States or the EMA (European Medicines Agency) in Europe. The analyses presented in the ISS and ISE help regulatory authorities evaluate the benefit-risk profile of the investigational drug and make informed decisions regarding its approval and labeling.

How to delete global macro?

In SAS, you can delete a global macro by using the %SYMDEL statement. This statement removes a macro variable from the global symbol table. Here's how you can delete a global macro:

%SYMDEL macro_name;
   Replace `macro_name` with the name of the macro variable you want to delete.
   Here's an example:

%let my_macro = This is a global macro;
%put &my_macro;
   %SYMDEL my_macro;
   %put &my_macro;
   In this example:
- We first define a global macro variable named `my_macro`.
- We then use `%put` to display the value of `my_macro`, which is "This is a global macro".
- Next, we use `%SYMDEL` to delete the `my_macro` macro variable.
- Finally, we use `%put` again to attempt to display the value of `my_macro`. Since the macro variable has been deleted, it will result in a blank output.

   It's important to note that once a macro variable is deleted using `%SYMDEL`, it cannot be retrieved, so use this statement carefully.

challenges while programming in ADaM (Analysis Data Model) datasets

When programming in ADaM (Analysis Data Model), several challenges may arise due to the complexity and rigor required to adhere to CDISC (Clinical Data Interchange Standards Consortium) standards and ensure accuracy and completeness in the analysis datasets. Here are some common challenges faced while doing ADaM programming, along with considerations to address them:

1. **Understanding the ADaM Specification**:
- Challenge: ADaM specifications can be complex documents with detailed requirements for analysis datasets.
- Consideration: Take time to thoroughly understand the ADaM specification document, paying close attention to variable definitions, derivations, formats, and labels.

2. **Applying Logic Carefully and Checking Values**:
- Challenge: Implementing complex logic for deriving variables accurately can lead to errors or discrepancies.
- Consideration: Double-check the logic used for variable derivations and validate the resulting values against expected outcomes. Use programming techniques such as data checks and conditional logic to ensure accuracy.

3. **Checking Log for Notes, Warnings, and Errors**:
- Challenge: Errors, warnings, or notes in the SAS log can indicate issues that need to be addressed.
- Consideration: Regularly review the SAS log for any messages and address them promptly. Errors must be resolved, warnings should be investigated, and notes should be reviewed for potential improvements.

4. **Cross-Checking with Mock Shells and CRF**:
- Challenge: Ensuring alignment between analysis datasets and mock shells or CRFs (Case Report Forms) can be challenging.
- Consideration: Cross-check analysis dataset variables with mock shells and CRFs to verify that all required variables are included and that their definitions match the specifications.

5. **Applying CDISC Rules for Variable Creation**:
- Challenge: Adhering to CDISC standards for variable naming conventions, formats, and classifications can be complex.
- Consideration: Follow CDISC rules and guidelines meticulously when creating new variables, ensuring consistency and compliance with industry standards.

6. **Applying Date Formats as per CDISC**:
- Challenge: Ensuring that date variables are formatted correctly according to CDISC standards.
- Consideration: Apply date formats precisely as specified in the CDISC standards, considering factors such as date formats, intervals, and special considerations for date variables.

7. **Applying Labels as per Specifications**:
- Challenge: Assigning appropriate labels to variables as per ADaM specifications.
- Consideration: Ensure that variable labels accurately reflect their meanings and are consistent with the definitions provided in the ADaM specification document.

8. **Ensuring Variables are in Uppercase**:
- Challenge: Maintaining consistency in variable naming conventions, including case sensitivity.

- Consideration: Convert all variable names to uppercase to ensure consistency and avoid issues related to case sensitivity in programming and data manipulation.

9. **Cross-Checking Merging of Different SDTM Datasets**:

- Challenge: Merging multiple SDTM (Study Data Tabulation Model) datasets to create analysis datasets can be complex, with potential issues related to merging keys and data integrity.

- Consideration: Thoroughly validate the merging process, cross-checking that all required variables are present, merging keys are consistent, and the resulting datasets maintain data integrity.

By addressing these challenges with careful attention to detail, thorough validation, and adherence to CDISC standards, ADaM programmers can ensure the accuracy, completeness, and compliance of analysis datasets used for regulatory submissions and clinical data analysis.

How do you annotate CRF

To annotate a CRF for SDTM effectively, the following steps are typically followed, incorporating the provided considerations:

1. **Review CRF**:
- Start by opening a blank CRF and marking each field with the corresponding variable name.

2. **Consult CDISC Implementation Guide and Client Reference Documents**:
- Refer to the CDISC Implementation Guide and any client-specific reference documents to ensure alignment with SDTM standards and guidelines.

3. **Annotate Information Exactly Suited for Variables**:
- Annotate each field in the CRF with information that corresponds exactly to SDTM variables as specified in the Implementation Guide.

4. **Use Different Colors for Different Domains**:
- Consider using different colors to annotate fields belonging to different SDTM domains for clarity and organization.

5. **Handle Missing Information**:
- If there is missing information for certain fields, annotate them as "Not Submitted" to indicate that data for those variables were not collected.

6. **Ensure Complete Annotation for Considered Domains**:
- Verify that all relevant information in the CRF has been annotated to correspond to SDTM domains, ensuring completeness.

7. **Map SDTM Program Based on Annotations**:
- Use the annotations to map the CRF data to SDTM domains programmatically, ensuring consistency and accuracy.

8. **Validate Annotations Before Release to Programmers**:
- Validate the annotations for accuracy and completeness before releasing them to programmers for SDTM conversion.

9. **Utilize Previous CRFs and Jira Tickets**:
- Draw on insights from previous CRFs and any Jira tickets raised during previous projects to improve the quality and completeness of the annotations.

10. **Allow Adequate Time for Annotation**:
- Allocate sufficient time, typically around one week, for the annotation process to ensure thoroughness and accuracy.

By following these steps and considerations, the CRF can be effectively annotated for SDTM mapping, supporting the conversion of data into SDTM format and ultimately facilitating regulatory submission and analysis in clinical research.

Phase1 Biomarkers , PK and PD

In Phase 1 clinical trials focused on biomarkers, pharmacokinetics (PK), and pharmacodynamics (PD), several key considerations and challenges arise.

1. **Study Design**:
- Designing Phase 1 trials to evaluate biomarkers, PK, and PD requires careful planning to determine the study population, dosing regimen, and endpoints relevant to the specific biomarkers and drug mechanisms.

2. **Biomarker Selection**:
- Identifying and selecting appropriate biomarkers that reflect the desired pharmacological effect or disease state targeted by the investigational drug is crucial. Biomarkers can include molecular, cellular, imaging, or physiological parameters.

3. **PK Assessments**:
- Conducting PK assessments involves studying the absorption, distribution, metabolism, and excretion (ADME) of the investigational drug in human subjects. PK parameters such as maximum concentration (Cmax), time to reach maximum concentration (Tmax), area under the curve (AUC), and half-life (t1/2) are evaluated.

4. **PD Assessments**:
- PD assessments focus on understanding the drug's effect on the body, including its mechanism of action, pharmacological activity, and potential therapeutic outcomes. PD biomarkers may include changes in physiological parameters, biomarker levels, or disease-related endpoints.

5. **Sample Collection and Analysis**:
- Collection, processing, and analysis of biological samples (e.g., blood, urine, tissue) for biomarker, PK, and PD assessments require standardized protocols and methodologies to ensure data quality and reliability.

6. **Data Integration and Analysis**:
- Integrating biomarker, PK, and PD data collected from Phase 1 trials involves comprehensive analysis to assess drug exposure, pharmacological effects, dose-response relationships, and safety profiles. Advanced statistical and modeling techniques may be employed for data interpretation.

7. **Safety Monitoring**:
- Monitoring safety parameters alongside biomarker, PK, and PD assessments is essential to evaluate the drug's safety profile, identify adverse events, and determine dose-limiting toxicities. Close monitoring of safety signals allows for timely intervention and dose adjustment if necessary.

8. **Regulatory Considerations**:
- Meeting regulatory requirements for biomarker, PK, and PD data submission is critical for obtaining regulatory approval. Ensuring compliance with regulatory guidelines and standards, such as FDA's Biomarker Qualification Program and CDISC SDTM standards, facilitates data review and regulatory decision-making.

9. **Interdisciplinary Collaboration**:
- Effective collaboration among clinicians, pharmacologists, biomarker scientists, statisticians, and regulatory experts is essential for the successful design, execution, and interpretation of Phase 1 trials focused on biomarkers, PK, and PD.

10. **Translation to Later Phases**:
- Insights gained from Phase 1 biomarker, PK, and PD studies inform subsequent clinical development phases,

guiding dose selection, patient stratification, efficacy assessments, and regulatory submissions in Phase 2 and Phase 3 trials.

Navigating Phase 1 trials focused on biomarkers, PK, and PD requires a comprehensive understanding of drug development principles, interdisciplinary collaboration, and adherence to regulatory standards to support the safe and effective development of new therapeutic interventions.

SE –How to derive SESTDTC and SEENDTC

In SDTM (Study Data Tabulation Model), SESTDTC (Start Date/Time of Subject Event) and SEENDTC (End Date/ Time of Subject Event) represent the onset and resolution dates/times of a subject event, respectively. These variables are derived from other variables collected during the study. Here's how you can derive SESTDTC and SEENDTC in SDTM:

1. **Deriving SESTDTC**:

- SESTDTC represents the start date/time of a subject event. It is typically derived from variables such as the event start date/time recorded in the CRF or dataset.

- If the CRF includes a specific field for the start date/time of the event (e.g., SESTDTC), you can directly map this field to SESTDTC in SDTM.

- If the event start date/time is recorded across multiple variables in the CRF (e.g., Date and Time separately), you may need to concatenate or combine these variables to form SESTDTC in the format specified by SDTM (e.g., ISO 8601 date/time format).

2. **Deriving SEENDTC**:

- SEENDTC represents the end date/time of a subject event, indicating when the event resolved or ended. Similar to SESTDTC, it is derived from variables collected in the study.

- If the CRF includes a specific field for the end date/time of the event (e.g., SEENDTC), you can map this field directly to SEENDTC in SDTM.

- If the event end date/time is recorded across multiple variables in the CRF, you may need to derive SEENDTC based on criteria such as the last observation date/time related to the event or any specific criteria defined in the study protocol.

- It's essential to ensure that SEENDTC is derived accurately, reflecting the resolution or end of the subject event without ambiguity.

3. **Considerations**:

- When deriving SESTDTC and SEENDTC, adhere to SDTM specifications regarding date/time formats, precision, and consistency.

- Validate derived values against the original data to ensure accuracy and consistency throughout the dataset.

- Document any derivation rules or transformations applied to derive SESTDTC and SEENDTC in the SDTM dataset's annotated CRF or data specifications.

By following these guidelines and considering the specific data collection practices and study protocols, you can accurately derive SESTDTC and SEENDTC in SDTM datasets, ensuring compliance with CDISC standards and facilitating the analysis and interpretation of subject event data in clinical research.

Epoch

In the context of clinical trials, an "epoch" refers to a predefined time interval used for organizing and analyzing data collected during the study. The concept of epochs is particularly relevant in longitudinal studies where data are collected at multiple time points over the course of the trial.

Here are some key points about epochs in clinical trials:

1. **Time Intervals**: An epoch represents a specific time interval during which data are collected or analyzed. The duration of each epoch can vary depending on the study design and objectives.

2. **Data Collection**: Clinical trial data, including clinical assessments, laboratory measurements, and patient-reported outcomes, are typically collected at specific time points corresponding to different epochs throughout the study.

3. **Data Analysis**: Data collected within each epoch may be analyzed separately or aggregated to evaluate treatment effects, safety outcomes, efficacy endpoints, or other study objectives.

4. **Endpoint Definition**: Epochs are often associated with predefined endpoints or assessment time points relevant to the study's primary and secondary objectives. For example, efficacy assessments may be conducted at specific epochs to evaluate treatment response over time.

5. **Statistical Analysis**: Statistical methods used for analyzing clinical trial data may involve comparing outcomes between treatment groups within each epoch, assessing trends over time, or modeling longitudinal data to characterize treatment effects.

6. **Adaptive Designs**: In adaptive clinical trial designs, epochs may be dynamically adjusted based on interim analyses or adaptive randomization procedures to optimize study efficiency or address emerging safety or efficacy signals.

7. **Regulatory Considerations**: Regulatory authorities such as the FDA and EMA may require sponsors to pre-specify epochs and endpoint analyses in the study protocol and statistical analysis plan submitted for regulatory approval.

Overall, epochs serve as a framework for organizing and analyzing longitudinal data in clinical trials, providing a structured approach to evaluating treatment effects and monitoring study outcomes over time.

SV - How you assign unscheduled visit

In clinical trials, unscheduled visits (SV) refer to visits by study participants that are not part of the planned visit schedule outlined in the study protocol. Assigning unscheduled visits involves capturing and documenting these visits in the clinical trial dataset. Here's how unscheduled visits can be assigned:

1. **Identification**:
- Study sites should identify unscheduled visits by participants through regular monitoring of participant interactions, patient diaries, or direct communication with study participants.

2. **Documentation**:
- Investigators or site staff should document details of unscheduled visits, including the reason for the visit, date and time of the visit, any procedures performed, and any adverse events or concomitant medications reported.

3. **CRF Completion**:
- Capture information about unscheduled visits in the Case Report Form (CRF) or electronic data capture (EDC) system used for data collection. Ensure that there is a designated section in the CRF to record unscheduled visits.

4. **Variable Assignment**:
- Assign appropriate variables in the dataset to capture information related to unscheduled visits. These variables may include:
- SVSTDTC: Start Date/Time of Unscheduled Visit
- SVENDTC: End Date/Time of Unscheduled Visit
- SVVISIT: Visit Name or Identifier for Unscheduled Visit
- SV...: Additional variables for capturing details such as reason for visit, procedures performed, and outcomes.

5. **Data Entry**:
- Enter data related to unscheduled visits accurately and promptly into the clinical trial database or EDC system to ensure timely capture of participant interactions and events.

6. **Data Review and Quality Control**:
- Implement data review and quality control procedures to verify the accuracy and completeness of information recorded for unscheduled visits. Perform reconciliations between source documents and entered data to identify discrepancies.

7. **Coding and Standardization**:
- Standardize the coding and classification of reasons for unscheduled visits using appropriate coding dictionaries or terminologies such as MedDRA (Medical Dictionary for Regulatory Activities) for adverse events or WHO Drug Dictionary for concomitant medications.

8. **Regulatory Compliance**:
- Ensure that the assignment and documentation of unscheduled visits comply with regulatory requirements and Good Clinical Practice (GCP) guidelines. Maintain documentation for auditing and regulatory inspection purposes.

By following these steps, clinical trial teams can effectively assign and document unscheduled visits, ensuring accurate capture of participant interactions and events throughout the study. This contributes to the integrity of the clinical trial data and supports the analysis and interpretation of study outcomes.

Is Death is derived or collected variable

In SDTM (Study Data Tabulation Model), "Death" is typically considered a collected variable rather than a derived one. "Death" refers to the occurrence of mortality or death of a study participant during the course of the clinical trial.

As a collected variable, information about death is typically recorded directly from the study participants' medical records, investigator assessments, or other sources of documentation. It is crucial to accurately capture and document details related to the death event, including the date of death, cause of death, and any relevant circumstances surrounding the event.

In SDTM datasets, variables related to death are typically included in domains such as "Adverse Events" (AE), "Medical History" (MH), or "Vital Signs" (VS), depending on the context and specifics of the study protocol. For example:

1. In the Adverse Events (AE) domain, variables such as "AEDECOD" (Adverse Event Preferred Term) may capture the cause of death, while "AESTDTC" (Adverse Event Start Date) may capture the date of death.

2. In the Medical History (MH) domain, variables such as "MHDECOD" (Medical History Decoded Term) may capture the cause of death, while "MHSTDTC" (Medical History Start Date) may capture the date of death.

3. In the Vital Signs (VS) domain, variables such as "VSDTC" (Vital Signs Date/Time) may capture the date of death, if applicable.

It's essential to follow SDTM implementation guidelines and ensure consistency in data collection, variable naming, and coding conventions when recording information about death events in clinical trial datasets. Additionally, adherence to regulatory requirements and Good Clinical Practice (GCP) guidelines is essential to maintain the integrity and reliability of the data.

Challenges faced during ISS and ISE

The challenges encountered during the creation of Integrated Summary of Safety (ISS) and Integrated Summary of Efficacy (ISE) documents in clinical trials can be multifaceted due to the complexity of integrating data from various studies and ensuring compliance with regulatory standards. Here's a framed question based on this topic:

"In the creation of Integrated Summary of Safety (ISS) and Integrated Summary of Efficacy (ISE) documents for clinical trials, what are some common challenges faced, and how can they be effectively managed?"

1. **Data Integration and Harmonization**:
- How do you manage the integration of safety and efficacy data from multiple studies conducted during a clinical trial program, considering variations in study designs and data collection methods?

2. **Ensuring Data Accuracy and Completeness**:
- What strategies do you employ to ensure the accuracy and completeness of safety and efficacy data included in the ISS and ISE documents, considering the critical nature of these analyses for regulatory submissions?

3. **Adherence to Regulatory Standards**:
- How do you ensure compliance with regulatory standards and guidelines, such as those provided by regulatory authorities like the FDA and EMA, when preparing ISS and ISE documents?

4. **Handling Missing or Incomplete Data**:
- How do you address challenges related to missing or incomplete data in safety and efficacy analyses, and what approaches do you use to mitigate potential biases in the analyses?

5. **Data Quality Control and Assurance**:
- What measures do you take to implement data quality control and assurance processes to identify and address data discrepancies, inconsistencies, or errors in ISS and ISE analyses?

6. **Cross-Study Variability and Heterogeneity**:
- How do you manage variability and heterogeneity across different studies included in the ISS and ISE analyses, and how do you ensure consistency in data interpretation and reporting?

7. **Statistical Analysis and Interpretation**:
- What statistical methodologies and approaches do you employ for the analysis of safety and efficacy data in ISS and ISE documents, and how do you interpret the results to support conclusions about the investigational product's safety and efficacy?

8. **Collaboration and Communication**:
- How do you facilitate effective collaboration and communication among multidisciplinary teams, including statisticians, clinicians, regulatory affairs experts, and medical writers, to ensure the successful preparation of ISS and ISE documents?

By addressing these challenges with careful planning, rigorous methodologies, and effective communication, clinical trial teams can navigate the complexities of preparing ISS and ISE documents and support the regulatory approval of investigational products.

why you are looking for job change?

Firstly, be clear over your reasons for changing jobs. Is it a step in career progression after you have learnt all that you could in your current job or are you <u>resigning</u> under unpleasant circumstances? Either way, they key to answering right is to sound positive, be crisp and concise, and definitely not beat around the bush if it's the latter case. Some concrete reasons can be

- A search for newer opportunities and challenges
- A chance to work in a <u>larger, more established organisation</u> or alternately a smaller start-up with greater responsibilities/learning curve.
- Shift in work domain
- Ah, this is a great (and very common) question. To begin, your interviewer is looking to see your response to determine your character. As a candidate, you should never use this question to bash your current or previous employer. Nor should you use this question to make yourself look bad by saying something like, 'I just couldn't handle it.' or 'I didn't like my co-workers'. **The best response is: 'I am looking for the experience that can prepare me better for my future as a _____. I have been told that your company is known for developing people professionally...ect. etc.'**